SAMUEL LANGHORNE CLEMENS (1835-1910) had recently adopted his famed pen name of "Mark Twain" shortly before he landed in the in 1866 Hawaiian Islands to spend four months as a correspondent for the most prominent newspaper on the Pacific Coast. When, in 1872; he needed to supplement the chapters in his personal narrative. *Roughing it* he drew upon his twenty-five articles for the Sacramento *Union* and his personal notes to supply the additional recollections here presented.

The views of the "Sandwich Islands" reported by America's most famous lecturer and beloved novelist in 1866 may differ somewhat from those of the visitor of the 1990's. "The Huckleberry Finn of foreign correspondents," however, gives many faithful accounts of old Honolulu, the nobility and their ceremonies, the City of Refuge on the Kona Coast, somnolent island of Maui, the native sport of surfriding, and the active volcano of Kilauea. And the light touch of the great humorist is seldom missing!

D0009258

MarkTwain
in

Roughing It in the Sandwich Islands

Foreword by
A. Grove Day

Mutual Publishing
Honolulu, Hawaii

Foreword "Innocent Abroad in Hawaii: Mark Twain" is
reprinted by permission from *Mad About Islands: Novelists of a
Vanished Pacific* (Mutual Publishing Co., Honolulu), copyright 1987
by A. Grove Day.
Illustrations courtesy of Bishop Museum, Hawaii State Archives, and
Robert E. Van Dyke Collection.

Cover design by Tamara Moan, Bechlen/Gonzalez, Inc.
ISBN 0-935189-93-1
Printed and bound in Australia by
The Book Printer, Victoria

"No alien land in all the world has any deep strong charm for me but that one, no other land could so longingly and so beseechingly haunt me, sleeping and walking, through half a lifetime, as that one has done. Other things leave me, but it abides; other things change, but it remains the same. For me its balmy airs are always blowing, its summer seas flashing in the sun; the pulsing of its surfbeat is in my ear, I can see its garlanded crags, its leaping cascades, its plumy palms drowsing by the shore, its remote summits floating like islands above the cloud wrack; I can feel the spirit of its woodland solitudes, I can hear the splash of its brooks; in my nostrils still lives the breath of flowers that perished twenty years ago."

Table of Contents

Once more upon the waters • our passengers • in the moonlight •
oranges and peaches • sugar plantations.

Foreword
Innocent Abroad in Hawaii:
Mark Twain

The future novelist of Hawaii got off the ship in Honolulu. He was thirty-one years old—not a novice, but not famous either. He had been handed the exotic assignment of writing a series of articles for the most important newspaper in the American West. It was his first venture outside his native land. He took his time, spending four months and one day inditing a series of twenty-five articles for the Sacramento *Union*. He was never to spend another day ashore in the islands, but he often looked back on his adventures there and years later began writing a novel with a Hawaiian setting. More than a century after his visit, what he wrote is still being collected in anthologies, used in advertisements, and quoted over dinner tables.

He was Samuel Langhorne Clemens (1835-1910), and he had only recently assumed the pen name of "Mark Twain." Quitting school at the age of twelve, this dropout of 1847 had obtained a sound education working in the family print-shop and helping to run the family newspaper. Before he reached his majority he had begun writing travel letters for the Keokuk *Post* under the signature of "Thomas Jefferson Snodgrass," and had published others during his days as a

professional Mississippi River pilot. He had adventured as
an irregular Confederate soldier, mountain prospector, and
Western newspaper reporter. He had seen his flawless tale,
"The Celebrated Jumping Frog of Calaveras County," published in a New York journal and reprinted around the
nation, but the journal had folded that same issue and his
first book would not be in print until three years in the future. Youngest of the surviving Clemenses, scapegrace Sam
was now the hope of his widowed, sixty-three-year-old
mother, his widowed sister, and his no-account elder brother
Orion. He had recently spent time in a San Francisco jail,
having commented too sharply on police brutality in that
city. One night earlier in the year he had put a pistol to his
head; many times later he was sorry his roulette game did not
succeed. No wonder he accepted an assignment that promised
a tropical interlude that, unknown to him, would, prove to
be a career watershed.

Sam's lifelong love affair with the future fiftieth state
began when the steamer *Ajax* arrived at Honolulu on
Sunday, March 18, 1866. His arrival was not noted in the
local press. He could not even get a room on his first night
ashore, but he was soon settled in the American Hotel,
where he paid seven dollars a week for a furnished room and
ten dollars for board.

A tireless sightseer, he began at once his reportorial
duties, riding around the capital island of Oahu on a spavined
horse. His first encounter with local merchants came when
he sought to obtain a drive-yourself steed. He found that
animal traders in Hawaii were even more shrewd than those
he had known in California. If the cheated buyer raised a
row, the dealer always had a "brother" who was responsible
but who had left for the country. One victim replied, "But I
know I hired the horse of you, because I noticed that scar on
your cheek." The rascal's answer was not bad: "Oh, yes—

yes—my brother all same—we twins!"

Aboard a languid animal he named "Oahu," the slight young man from Missouri, with drooping mustache and flaming red hair, was usually garbed in a starched, brown linen duster that reached to his ankles. He talked and gesticulated so violently that strangers thought he was always drunk; but he was merely gathering news. He was accompanied in his imagination by his mythical friend Mr. Brown, who got the blame in the newspaper letters for all the crude remarks that even Mark Twain did not dare to utter.

The series of letters from Hawaii, had they been collected for hardbound publication, would have been Mark Twain's first book. Today they are available in libraries in no fewer than eight reprinted editions. They constitute the author's most important contribution to the literature of the Hawaiian Islands, which in his time were usually referred to as the "Sandwich Islands," the name bestowed by Captain James Cook, first European to give the outside world an account of these remote regions of the Pacific.

The letters, printed in both the daily and weekly editions of the Sacramento Union, are excellent reportage by a keen-eyed man who all his life was a calculating observer of the universe around him. They cover not only the sugar and whaling industries, which were of interest to American businessmen of the time, but also the Hawaiian export trade, which brought high fees to the United States Customs. The letters are laden with dozens of descriptions that offer a strong contrast with the highrise, traffic-jammed Americanized scenes of today. The rutted streets were thronged with few tourists but with jostling people of a dozen nations, bartering for hay or fish or poi. Much of the material deals with scenery and climate, politics, social conditions, history and legends, Polynesian lore, the royal family of the kingdom, religious affairs, and even the "millions of cats" of Honolulu. As might be expected of the writer who became America's greatest comic genius, the letters are sprinkled with humor. They are also laden with dozens of descriptions of scenic features of the islands that are still landmarks today. If we make proper allowance for the calculated exaggerations for which Twain was famous, one can recommend a close reading of these Sandwich Islands letters to anyone who wishes a frank and sometimes violent view of Hawaii in the reign of the fifth Kamehameha. And, as will be mentioned, Mark Twain also added to the literature of Hawaii with a number of chapters in his book *Roughing It*— not to mention copious jottings in his 1866 notebooks.

Residents of the metropolis of Honolulu today might rejoice in the Clemens description of the capital. "The town of Honolulu (said to contain between twelve thousand and fifteen thousand inhabitants) is spread over a dead level; has streets from twenty to thirty feet wide, solid and level as a floor, most of them straight as a line and a few as crooked as a corkscrew; houses one and two stories high, built of wood, straw, 'dobes, and dull cream-colored pebble-and-shell-conglomerated coral cut into oblong square blocks and laid in cement, but no brick houses; there are great yards, more like plazas, about a large number of the dwelling houses, and these are carpeted with bright green grass, into which your foot sinks out of sight; and they are ornamented by a hundred species of beautiful flowers and blossoming shrubs, and shaded by noble tamarind trees and the 'Pride of India,' with its fragrant flower, and by the 'Umbrella Tree,' and I do not know how many more. I had rather smell Honolulu at sunset than the old police courtroom in San Francisco."

Californians of today may not know that, in the era of their gold rush, oranges were shipped to the Coast from Hawaii. In the tropics, Mark Twain felt the need of fruit and indulged himself. "You pay about twenty-five cents . . . a dozen for oranges; and so delicious are they that some people frequently eat a good many at luncheon. I seldom eat more than ten or fifteen at a sitting, however, because I despise to see anybody gourmandize. . . . Bananas are worth about a bit [12-1/2 cents] a dozen—enough for that overrated fruit. Strawberries are plenty, and as cheap as the bananas. . . . I have a kind of general idea that the tamarinds are rather sour this year. I had a curiosity to taste these things, and I knocked half a dozen off the tree and ate them the other day. They sharpened my teeth up like a razor, and put a 'wire edge' on them that I think likely will wear off when the enamel does."

Not averse to a slug of whisky over a Western bar, Mark noted the temperance atmosphere that came in with the missionaries of 1820 and was to linger for more than a century. "I have said that the wines and liquors sold here are not of the best quality. It could not well be otherwise, as I can show. There seem to be no hard, regular drinkers in this town, or at least very few; you perceive that the duties are high; saloonkeepers pay a license of a thousand dollars a year; they must close up at ten o'clock at night and not open again before daylight the next morning; they are not allowed to open on Sunday at all. These laws are very strict, and are rigidly obeyed."

The drinks, when found, usually lacked cooling chunks of ice. "Ice is worth a hundred dollars a ton in San Francisco, and five or six hundred here, and if the steamer [the *Ajax*] continues to run, a profitable trade may possibly be driven in the article hereafter. It does not pay to bring from Sitka in sailing vessels, though. It has be tried. It proved a mutinous and demoralizing cargo, too; for the sailors drank the melted freight and got so high-toned that they refused ever afterwards to go to sea unless the captains would guarantee them ice water on the voyage." This information, of course, came from the ubiquitous Mr. Brown.

In three different letters Twain mentions the menace to traffic caused by careering Hawaii horseback riders, especially on Saturday afternoons. "The native girls by twos and threes and parties of a dozen, and sometimes in whole platoons and companies, went cantering up and down the neighboring streets astride of fleet but homely horses, and with their gaudy riding habits streaming like banners behind them. Such a troop of free and easy riders, in their natural home, which is the saddle, makes a gay and graceful and exhilarating spectacle. . . . The girls put on all their finery they can scare up on Saturday afternoon—fine black silk robes; flowing red ones that nearly put your eyes out; others as white as snow; still others that discount the rainbow; and they wear their hair in nets, and trim their jaunty hats with fresh flowers, and encircle their dusky throats with home-made necklaces of the brilliant vermilion-tinted blossom of the ohia; and they fill the markets and the adjacent streets with their bright presences, and smell like thunder with their villainous coconut oil."

Mark attended a hula show and mourned the decline of the ancient ceremonial and religious performance, which he labeled "the lascivious dance that was wont to set the passions of men ablaze in the old heathen days, a century ago." And considering the penal conditions on Oahu in later days, it is a paradox that the reporter thought the jail was "the pleasantest quarters in Honolulu" and "the model prison of the Western half of the world."

Twain also described the royal palace—"a large, roomy frame building"—and a session of the legislature, which he concluded was no more stupid than similar bodies elsewhere. He especially was impressed by the actions of the translator, Bill Ragsdale, who was later to be chosen as the model for the protagonist of Twain's projected Hawaii novel.

"At 11 a.m. His Royal Highness the President called the house to order. The roll call was dispensed with for some reason or other, and the chaplain, a venerable looking white man, offered up a prayer in the native tongue; and I must say that this curious language, with its numerous vowels and its entire absence of hissing sounds, fell very softly and musically from his lips. A white chief clerk read the journal of the preceding day's proceedings in English, and then handed the document to Bill Ragsdale, a 'half white' (half white and half Kanaka), who translated and clattered it off in Kanaka with a volubility that was calculated to make a slow-spoken man like me distressingly nervous. . . . There is a spice of deviltry in the fellow's nature, and it crops out every now and then when he is translating the speeches of slow old Kanakas who do not understand English. Without departing from the spirit of a member's remarks, he will, with apparent unconsciousness, drop in a little voluntary contribution occasionally in the way of a word or two that will make the gravest speech utterly ridiculous. He is careful not to venture upon such experiments, though, with the remarks of persons able to detect him. I noticed when he translated for his Excellency David Kalakaua, who is an accomplished English scholar, he asked, 'Did I translate you correctly, Your Excellency?' The rascal."

Mark Twain, who had served as a legislative reporter in the Territory of Nevada, pictured a member from another Hawaiian island getting up and gravely offering a bill for "the construction of a suspension bridge from Oahu to Hawaii, a matter of a hundred and fifty miles! He said that natives would prefer it to the interisland schooners, and they wouldn't suffer seasickness on it. . . . Do not do an unjust thing now, and imagine Kanaka legislatures do stupider things than other similar bodies. Rather blush to remember that once, when a Wisconsin legislature had the affixing of a penalty for the crime of arson under consideration, a member got up and seriously suggested that when a man committed the damning crime of arson they ought either to hang him or make him marry the girl"

Mark Twain described for his California readers a number of prominent figures in the post-Civil War Kingdom of Hawaii. He gave sketches of the two possible successors to the throne after the current monarch passed away—Prince William C. Lunalilo and David Kalakaua, both of whom were to be elected to the kingship, the former in 1873 and the latter a year later. Twain noted at length the month-long obsequies and national mourning at the death of Princess Victoria Kamamalu. His verbal portrait of the reigning ruler, Lot Kamehameha V, is well worth recording.

"The King is thirty-four years of age, it is said, but looks all of fifty. He has an observant, inquiring eye, a heavy, massive face, a lighter complexion than is common with his race, tolerably short, stiff hair, a moderate mustache and imperial, large stature, inclining somewhat to corpulence, . . . has fleshy hands, but a small foot for his size, is about six feet high, is thoughtful and slow of movement, has a large head, firmly set upon broad shoulders, and is a better man and a better looking one than he is represented to be in the villainous popular photographs of him, for none of them are good." Some time later, in a letter appearing in the New York *Daily Tribune* of January 9, 1873, in which Twain favored annexation of the islands by the United States, he recalled: "There was no trivial royal nonsense about him; he dressed plainly, poked about Honolulu, night and day, on his old horse, unattended; he was popular, greatly respected, and even beloved."

Missionary activities were also topics for the journalist. Although he remarked in his *Notebook*, "More missionaries and more row about saving these 60,000 people than would take to convert hell itself," it is clear that Twain felt the Christian, democratic order in the islands was infinitely better than the old pagan feudalism that it had endeavored to replace. He had a good word to say also for the Roman Catholic Mission under Bishop L.D. Maigret. But he felt that the incursion of the Church of England, founded in Honolulu in 1862 under royal British auspices, was unnecessary. He reserved his most choice invective for Bishop T.N. Staley and the lanky American finance minister, C.C. Harris, who, said Twain, belonged "body and soul, and boots, to the King of the Sandwich Islands and the `Lord Bishop of Honolulu.'"

At the end of his twelfth letter, the reporter confessed that he had not touched a pen for six weeks. He had gone to visit the somnolent island of Maui, intending to stay for a week. He stayed for five, and in later life remembered Maui as the dream refuge from pressures of life as a celebrity.

He made up for his slackness toward the end of June, when in Letter 15 he sent off a lengthy first account of a notable sea tragedy. It was a journalist's dream scoop. His story was to be headlined "Burning of the Clipper Ship *Hornet* at Sea." To the wandering correspondent had come a chance to reveal one of the most amazing incidents in the chronicles of the ocean.

The ship *Hornet*, commanded by Captain Josiah A. Mitchell, caught fire near the equator south of Hawaii, from an explosion which resulted when one of the mates, against orders, went below with an open light to draw a can of varnish. The crew abandoned the ship in such haste that holes were staved in the boats in which they had to embark on a bitter voyage from which half of them did not return.

Captain Mitchell and fourteen of his men arrived in the longboat at Laupahoehoe, a village on the shore of the island of Hawaii, after a forty-three-day open-boat ordeal in which they voyaged four thousand miles. Lack of food and tight rationing of water had caused a conspiracy, intent on cannibalism, against the captain, who dared not sleep for fear of mutiny. James Norman Hall, in a footnote to his *The Tale of a Shipwreck*, calls the achievement of Captain Mitchell "fully as heroic as that performed by Captain Bligh and the *Bounty*'s men, and, in some respects, even more remarkable."

When some of the rescued seamen were brought to a hospital in Honolulu, Mark Twain himself was laid up in his lodgings with saddle boils. But his recent acquaintance, Anson Burlingame, on his way to serve as United States minister to China, arranged to have Twain carried in his cot to the hospital. There Burlingame questioned the survivors and Twain took notes for the article which he sat up all night to write. Next morning the manuscript of this longest of the letters to the *Union* was tossed aboard a schooner which had already cast off for San Francisco.

This front-page story was the first full report of the disaster to reach the United States and was widely reprinted. On his return to California, Twain boldly billed his newspaper for $300, a sum fifteen times the usual $20 paid for his letters. He later used the *Hornet* material for two other articles: "Forty-three Days in an Open Boat" (*Harper's Magazine*, December, 1866) and "My Debut as a Literary Person" (*Century Magazine*, November, 1899).

In July, Mark Twain embarked on an interisland schooner he called the *Boomerang*, heading for a tour of the Big Island of Hawaii. He suffered the rigors of the sea trip to the full, as witness his evocative account of sailing to the Kona Coast in this pitching schooner overloaded with people, dogs, mats, calabashes of poi, saddles, and man-eating cockroaches. He devoted no less than four letters to the Kona region, mentioning the legend of the god Lono, the City of Refuge at Napoopoo, the temple where Henry Obookiah (the model

Hawaiian youth that Sam Clemens had heard about in Sunday school) had served a pagan priest, and the monument to Captain Cook at Kealakekua Bay. At that time, the spot where the discoverer had been killed by his disillusioned worshippers was commemorated only by an ancient coconut stump on which were nailed various metal plates marking the visits of other British voyagers, such as Lord George Paulet (Twain, the proud American, had some harsh remarks to emit concerning Cook, Paulet, and Richard Chariton, former British consul). To fill out part of a letter, Mark indulged himself in a humorous scene in which he catches Mr. Brown, his souvenir-hunting comrade, trying to drag away the stump and take it back to show the folks at home.

Further travels included a journey around the southern end of Hawaii—where at Waiohinu he is reputed to have planted a monkeypod tree that grew to immense size before it blew down in a windstorm in 1957. He then headed for the Kilauea Volcano district, which gave him plenty of material for half a dozen impassioned final pages in his final letter. Then, after viewing the sugar plantations of the Hamakua region, he rode along the deep gash of Waipio Valley, crossed the Waimea tableland, and caught the little steamer *Kilauea* at Kawaihae for his return to Honolulu.

Dates given at the heads of letters cannot always be fully trusted. The last eight letters were published after Mark's return to California, and some of them were written after his return and dated earlier. Letter Twenty-three was dated "Honolulu, September 10," nearly a month after he was back in San Francisco. The last letter, dated "Volcano House, June 3d—Midnight," was published on November 16, and gave the date of his stay at the volcano rather than the date he wrote the letter that wound up the series.

Some years later, when Mark Twain needed to fill out his book on Western travel, *Roughing It* (1872), he wrote

Chapters Seventy-four through Seventy-eight by drawing upon the ninety thousand words of his *Union* letters about Hawaii. These chapters in *Roughing It* (omitted in most later reprints) used thirty thousand words from the letters and added some five thousand words of new material, describing how he got down the volcano and back home. Some of the material in the letters was left out of the book because it was too spirited, for when part of it was reprinted some time later in the Honolulu newspapers, a great stir resulted locally.

The shorter, later version of the Hawaiian adventures in *Roughing It* is smoothly written and artfully told, and the crude Mr. Brown does not appear. A good example of this style is found in the passage about Mark's explorations in the volcano region. Although the fire pit of Halemaumau was not in violent eruption at the time, Twain's account states that Vesuvius was "a mere toy, a child's volcano, a soup kettle" by comparison. He also describes a harrowing hike in darkness, lighted only by eruptive flares, across the bottom of the pit, when straying a few inches off the invisible path might plunge the reporter and his comrade into chasms below the rotten lava crust. Few island spots still of interest, in fact, were left unvisited by this keen-eyed journalist of the century past.

Oddly, Twain did not mention in his letters the sport of surfboard riding, which had been practiced long before Captain Cook dropped anchor at Kealakekua. But in *Roughing It* he recalled his experiences while learning to surf on the Big Island. "In one place," he wrote, "we came upon a large company of naked natives, of both sexes and all ages, amusing themselves with the national pastime of surfbathing. Each heathen would paddle three or four hundred yards out to sea (taking a short board with him), then face the shore and wait for a particularly prodigious billow to come along; at the right moment he would fling his board upon its foamy crest and himself upon the board, and here he would come whizzing by like a bombshell! It did not seem that a lightning express-train could shoot along at a more hair-lifting speed. I tried surf-bathing once, subsequently, but made a failure of it. I got the board placed right, and at the right moment, too; but missed the connection myself. The board struck the shore in three-quarters of a second, without any cargo, and I struck the bottom about the same time, with a couple of barrels of water in me. None but natives ever master the art of surf-bathing thoroughly."

Mark Twain's first travels abroad resulted not only in an amazing collection of contemporary accounts but also an early prophecy of what America's role in the Pacific was to become during the century ahead of him. "To America has been vouchsafed to materialize the vision, and realize the dream of centuries, of the enthusiasts of the Old World. We have found the true and only direct route to the bursting coffers of `Ormus and of Ind'—to the enchanted land whose mere drippings in the ages that are gone enriched and aggrandized ancient Venice, first, then Portugal, Holland, and in our own time England—and each in succession they longed and sought for the fountainhead of this vast Oriental wealth, and sought in vain. The path was hidden to them, but we have found it over the waves of the Pacific, and American enterprise will penetrate to the heart and center of its hoarded treasures, its imperial affluence." What other writer at this early date better glimpsed the role of America in Asia and in the Pacific, ocean of the future?

It is likely that only scholars of Hawaiian literature will be interested in Mark Twain's notebook entries, put down during his 1866 trip. These were published in complete form in 1975 and extensively annotated in the fine series issued by the University of California Press.

It is of interest, however, to read in an early entry that "Whalers like Kanakas better than any other sailors—temperate, strong, faithful, peaceable & orderly." Twain also writes that "Country will eventually pass into hands of foreigners—probably French"; but a page or two later he remarks: "English striving hard for supremacy—former King [Kamehameha I] favored them—present favors America." He does not mention in his letters the dread disease of leprosy, probably feeling that such a topic would discourage foreign investment; but he did visit the receiving hospital at Kalihi on June 29. Anson Burlingame's nineteen year-old son Ed was apparently the originator of the Biblical parody—"If a man ask thee to go with him a mile, go with him, Twain"—a joke that later became painfully trite. Concerning American annexation, a possibility discussed as early as 1866, there are two notes: "Americans want annexation, of course, to get rid of duties" and "It would be fair to have reciprocity anyway—then—no duties at either end, Cal would have S.I. trade." Concerning the local blue laws, Twain writes: "In Kona, natives make living watching for adultery—fine $30 each." Concerning the sugar-cane crop, he writes: "Matures in 12 mos & always tassels in November—rattoons the same of course—some of present crop is 3d rattoon." Finally, a note on Twain's note about local newspaper circulations quotes a later claim by Henry Whitney, editor, that he refused Twain a job as reporter on the *Pacific Commercial Advertiser* "reputedly on suspicion of laziness."

Mark Twain departed from the islands on July 19 on the sailing vessel *Smyrniote*. Arriving in San Francisco without funds, he was persuaded to earn some money by giving a lecture at the Academy of Music in that city on October 2, 1866. The announcement ended: "Doors open at 7 o'clock;

the trouble begins at 8." The topic was later to be billed as "Our Fellow Savages of the Sandwich Islands." Almost collapsing with stage fright, Mark nevertheless put on a performance that was greeted with uproarious enthusiasm. Thereafter, as he said, "I have always been able to gain my living without doing any work." Although teaching himself to become the foremost public speaker of his time was actually very hard work, lecturing—expanded to include readings from his works and after-dinner commentating—became a profession for him second only to that of authorship.

The Sandwich Islands lecture became his favorite. He used it through the winter of 1866-1867; it was the tour lecture for the season of 1873-1874 in England and the United States. In the latter version the influence is most apparent of a book that Mark Twain borrowed from the library of "Father" Samuel Chenery Damon's Mission in Honolulu (and tardily returned). This volume, which Mark read soon after his arrival, along with histories by Henry Theodore Cheever, Manley Hopkins, and Sheldon Dibble, was *History of the Hawaiian Islands* by James Jackson Jarves. A Bostonian who first arrived in Hawaii at the age of nineteen, Jarves became a merchant, planter, editor, and author not only of history books but of *Kaiana*, the first novel in English with a Hawaiian setting. Mark Twain was to make excellent use of that library book some years later, not merely for lecturing purposes.

Many times during his life, Samuel L. Clemens yearned to revisit the islands to which, as Albert Bigelow Paine claimed, the author always planned "to return some day, to stay there until he died." In a letter of October 26, 1881, to his friend Charles Warren Stoddard in Hawaii, he wrote: "If the house would only burn down, we would pack up the cubs and fly to the isles of the blest, and shut ourselves up in the healing solitudes of Haleakala and get a good rest; for the

mails do not intrude there, nor yet the telephone and the
telegraph. And after resting, we would come down the
mountain a piece and board with a godly, breech-clouted
native, and eat poi and dirt and give thanks to whom all
thanks belong, for these privileges, and never house-keep
any more. . . . What I have always longed for was the privilege of living forever away up on one of those mountains in
the Sandwich Islands overlooking the sea."

Twain dreamed for almost thirty years of returning to the
paradise he remembered. He was destined to get a tan-
talizing glimpse of Honolulu again in 1895, when he was on
a globe-girdling lecture trip designed to repay the creditors
who had lost money in his financial collapse of that year.
First stop in the Pacific was Hawaii, and from the deck of the
steamer *Warrimoo* Mark once more sighted Diamond Head,
but was not allowed to go ashore because a plague of cholera
had broken out in the city that had become the capital of
the Republic of Hawaii. The third chapter of Twain's
Following the Equator (1897) tells of this disappointment and
is an additional bit of Hawaiiana by the author that William
Dean Howells termed "the Lincoln of our literature." Mark
Twain was to discover that his first excursion out of his
native United States would bring him pleasure and fame. It
furnished him with a much-needed period of refreshment
after a jading career in Western America; it provided material
for a series of popular travel accounts anticipating those
later made into his first published book, *The Innocents Abroad*;
it gave him a journalistic scoop that made him a "literary
personage". it started him on a new and lucrative profession—
that of lecturer; and it supplied a setting for a contemplated
novel. Where is that novel now?

Many admirers of Mark Twain do not know that in 1884
he was at work on a novel about Hawaii. He wrote to his

close friend William Dean Howells on October 7: "My billiard table is stacked up with books relating to the Sandwich Islands; the walls are upholstered with scraps of paper pencilled with notes drawn from them. I have saturated myself with knowledge of that unimaginably beautiful land and that most strange and fascinating people. And I have begun a story.

"Its hidden motive will illustrate a but little considered fact in human nature; that the religious folly you are born in you will *die* in, no matter what apparently reasonabler religious folly may seem to have taken its place meanwhile and abolished and obliterated it. I start with Bill Ragsdale at 12 years of age, and the heroine at 4, in the midst of the ancient idolatrous system, with its picturesque and amazing customs and superstitions, 3 months before the arrival of the missionaries and the erection of a shallow Christianity upon the ruins of the old paganism. Then these two will become educated Christians, and highly civilized.

And then I will jump 15 years, and do Bill Ragsdale's leper business. When we come to dramatize, we can draw a deal of matter from the story, all ready to our hand." Like other visitors to Hawaii, such as Robert Louis Stevenson, Jack London, and James A. Michener, Twain was enchanted by the drama of the old isolation colony where the actual Bill Ragsdale, like many another unfortunate, came to a sad end.

In *Following the Equator*, Twain gave further information about Ragsdale, the former interpreter at the legislature. His prosperous career was cut short, just as he was about to marry a part-white girl, when he discovered that he had been stricken with leprosy. Although he could have concealed his plight for some years, he refused to marry and, cutting loose from family and friends, volunteered to immure himself on the ghastly shore of the island of Molokai. He arrived there previous to the ministrations of the notable Father Damien de Veuster, and "died the loathsome, lingering death that all lepers die."

The Hawaii novel was presumably never completed. Paine in his collection of Twain's *Letters* says that the author never finished the story, but in letters of January 24 and 30, 1884, to Twain's friend Mrs. Fairbanks, Twain said he had finished it and was about to give it a "most painstaking revision." Moreover, in a letter of February 25 of the same year, he asked Howells if he had yet blocked out the Sandwich Islands play—as if he had sent the story to Howells for the purpose of making it into a drama.

A visitor to the Mark Twain Collection at the University of California Library at Berkeley may view seventeen pages of manuscript of this novel, of which nine contain a rather ornate description of the islands. A brief fragment consists of a dialogue between the king and a boy whose sister has been threatened with death, but is released. A third fragment, in the words of Dr. Henry Nash Smith, former custodian of the collection, "obviously humor, reports an incident in which the king's spittoon has been stolen, to the consternation of the priests and the people generally."

The following selection from the opening of the novel's draft might be thought to rival the later and more famous prose poem":

"The date is 1840. Scene the true Isles of the Blest; that is to say, the Sandwich Isles—to this day the peacefullest, restfullest, sunniest, balmiest, dreamiest haven of refuge for a worn and weary spirit the surface of the earth can offer. Away out there in the mid-solitudes of the vast Pacific, and far down to the edge of the tropics, they lie asleep on the waves, perpetually green and beautiful, remote from the work-day world and its frets and worries, a bloomy, fragrant paradise, where the troubled may go and find peace, and the sick and tired find strength and rest. There they lie, the divine islands, forever shining in the sun, forever smiling out on the sparkling sea, with its soft mottlings of drifting cloud-shadows and vagrant cat's-paws of wind; forever inviting you, never repulsing you; and whosoever looks upon them once will never more get the picture out of his memory till he die. With him it will stay, and be always present; always present and always fresh; neither time nor distance can dim its features, or dull their charm, or reconcile him to the thought that he will never see that picture with his eyes of flesh again."

What happened to the rest of this manuscript? Some writers, such as Tom Horton in *Honolulu* magazine, have made its disappearance a topic that not even the combined efforts of Sherlock Holmes and Dr. Watson could solve. Nor is there any use hoping that a tattered manuscript of Mark Twain's Hawaii novel will someday be discovered in a New England hayloft. Although the Sandwich Islands novel that Twain was excitedly working on in 1884 has vanished, the mystery of its disappearance was solved many years ago by an American teacher in the Middle West. Much of its material, he reveals, and not a few of its main ideas, were finally incorporated into a newer novel—the author's most effective satire, *A Connecticut Yankee in King Arthur's Court* (1889).

Professor Fred W. Lorch's article in *American Literature* in March, 1958, attempts to show "that many of the basic concepts of feudal society and its practices which come under attack in the *Yankee* had their inception on Mark Twain's early observations of life in the Sandwich Islands, and particularly in his wide reading of Sandwich Islands history." Twain's borrowed copy of Jarves' history would now come into play; in fact, as Lorch says, the use of the tabu system by the Hawaiian priests was compared by Jarves to the interdict of the church of Rome, and of course at the end of the *Yankee* novel the dread interdict defeats The Boss's republican plans.

"It will be seen," adds Lorch, "that Mark Twain's indictment of the social, political, and religious practices in the islands is strikingly similar to his indictment of these same practices in King Arthur's England. And no less remarkable is the similarity between the role of the American missionaries who destroyed the old order in the Sandwich Islands and the role of the Connecticut Yankee who sought to free King Arthur's serfs in much the same way."

The Lorch article also attempts to show "that to an important degree the *Yankee* sprang out of the tail of a Sandwich Islands novel he was busily at work on in the winter and spring of 1883-1884, immediately prior to the time he came upon Malory's *Morte d'Arthur*."

The great work attributed to Sir Thomas Malory, along with the *Don Quixote* of Cervantes, is usually presumed to be a major influence on the celebrated *Yankee* novel, a popular success not only in fiction but also in films and even as a Broadway musical. If we follow the Lorch argument, however, his theme becomes stronger and stronger in conviction.

Most of us have had occasional reveries in which we dream that a person who has mastered today's state-of-the-art technology could return in a time machine to a "primitive" society in which he could astound the natives by displays of apparent magic. Would he ascend to power through this modern knowledge? Or would he, perhaps, be immediately sacrificed as an evil sorcerer?

Mark Twain's apparent answer in his puzzling *Yankee* book is that a skilled mechanic of his own time and place could quickly subdue all doubts in an early British feudal community, but that after a few years of "modernization," the old forces of reaction would eventually lead to Armageddon.

The novelist here was following tradition, in that both Arthur's sixth-century Celtic resisters of encroaching Continental forces and the courtly fourteenth-century knightly bands who engaged in chivalric tourneys in northern Europe were overthrown in the end by treachery from within or circumstances without. The Camelot of Geoffrey of Monmouth and the Camelot of Sir Thomas Malory, separated as they are by centuries, both agreed that "progress" could not last indefinitely. Even Lord Tennyson in his *Idylls of the King* concludes that "The old order changeth, yielding place to new;/And God fulfills himself in many ways,/Lest one good custom should corrupt the world." Change is not only inevitable but necessary, and those who live by technology are doomed to die by technology.

This digression may be far afield from the Honolulu of 1866. It is needed, however, to appreciate Professor Lorch's reasons why he thinks that Mark Twain's Hawaii novel was transformed into an attack on the nineteenth-century materialism of "the Gilded Age"—as Twain himself labeled it. On the evidence of Twain's letters to Howells and Mrs. Fairbanks, the manuscript fragments in Berkeley, and the author's remarks here and there about Bill Ragsdale, one can deduce what the Hawaii novel was to contain and what its tone would be.

The tone, although apparently comic, is serious in the main, and the ending is misery and suicide. Ragsdale's life was tragic, and his real-life role as prototype of Hank Morgan in the *Yankee* story was certainly not as a figure of burlesque.

At last we can come to Lorch's arguments to show how a planned novel became a different novel. First, since the planned one starts in 1819, three months before the coming of the New England missionaries and "in the midst of the ancient idolatrous system," and then continues on until a shallow Christianity has been erected, Mark Twain's story would inevitably have shown a contrast between the old Hawaiian civilization and the new. This contrast would have involved not only customs and superstitions—including the dreaded tabus—but also the oppressive power of kings, chiefs, and priests.

Second, he would have shown the progress of converting and civilizing the Hawaiian people and shown the work of the missionaries, their efforts and rebuffs. Hank Morgan, the Yankee, is obviously a missionary of modernism, and in the Camelot novel the soap salesmen on bicycles are referred to as "missionaries."

Third, he would have emphasized the strength of the old superstitions and practices, and how these in the end would cause Bill Ragsdale to backslide under the horrors of the leper colony on Molokai.

Finally, although the novel would be seriously intended, he would not have overlooked the chance to burlesque some of the ancient customs, such as having a court official collect the saliva of the ruler to protect him from sorcery. He would not, however, have satirized the missionaries themselves, for these were the ones who brought the light of religion and civilization to the islands. Looking back, few historians of today would dare to declare that the influences of pre-1820 in Hawaii, such as the traders and whalemen, should be preferred to the efforts of the New Englanders who brought to the pagans the *palapala* as well as the *pule* education along with prayer. Mark Twain felt that the Christian, democratic order of his century was certainly better than the feudalism of the sixth in Britain or the seventeenth in Hawaii. As James A. Michener once remarked: "Hiram Bingham [leader of the 1820 mission pioneers] is one of the most difficult great men of history to love, but everyone looking at either Hawaii or the Pacific is required either to stand for Bingham, the bigoted Old Testament figure, or those other Americans who almost destroyed the islands."

Other echoes of Hawaiian history can be found in the *Yankee* tale. Before the final battle, as Lorch notes, Morgan's right-hand man selects, as an elite squadron, a band of boys, none younger than fourteen and none above seventeen, who would have never been inculcated with the priestly superstitions. The other men would be sure to desert to the simple faith in which they were born. Bill Ragsdale must surely have abandoned his superficial Christianity and died in the creed in which he was born. The training of future fighters for freedom in Camelot is paralleled by the fact that the Hawaiian missionaries screened native applicants for church membership. The episode of the smallpox hut could have been drawn from the novelist's reading of the Hawaii historians and the horrors of pre-Damien Molokai.

The depiction of Merlin as an evil magician is not found in Malory, where he is a benevolent agent of the chivalric ideal. A villain was needed for the novel, of course, but Mark's Merlin bears more than one resemblance to the descriptions in Jarves and others of the rapacity of the island *kahuna anaana*, or sorcerer. Again, the inconstancy and incontinence of the women of King Arthur's court reflects many observations by visitors to the islands whose ships were besieged by swimming maidens anxious to offer their charms to any male in the offing. As Lorch remarks, "Nothing gave the missionaries more trouble than the establishment of Christian standards of sexual morality."

Lorch does not draw any parallels between Twain's portrait of King Arthur and his several sketches of Kamehameha V of the Kingdom of Hawaii. But after all, the first reigning monarch that democratic Mark Twain ever met was the man he described in his Letter Thirteen and his newspaper letter of January 9, 1873. There are places in the novel where King Arthur does somewhat resemble King Lot Kame-hameha.

Early critics were surprised that Mark Twain was able to deliver the manuscript of *A Connecticut Yankee* in what was for him a quite brief time. He was heavily occupied in seeing his *Huckleberry Finn* volume through the press, along with involvement in various business enterprises—especially his attempt to have completed a working model of the baffling Paige Typesetter, a bankrupting invention he dreamed would replace human compositors for the press. One answer is that the main outlines of his story had been mulled over in his mind for many years. The effort to become a millionaire through marketing a revolutionary patent in the printing industry (a trade in which he had been engaged since childhood) was a missionary expedition of his own.

"I want to finish [the book] the day the machine finishes," he kept saying. He finished the book in May, 1889, but the machine was never finished. And when the machine failed, the author swung as always to extremes. In his novel he depicted a world in which the machine civilization of American capitalist democracy would symbolically collapse into an economic Armageddon. As his best biographer, Justin Kaplan, wrote: "The ambivalences, disillusions, destructive fury, and, finally, homicidal tantrums of the novel were fire drills in his imagination for the actual failure of the machine, machine values, and his dream of capitalist democracy in which he expected to be a tycoon among tycoons."

The most frequently quoted slogan in Hawaiian literature is Mark Twain's description of the group as :the loveliest fleet of islands that lies anchored in any ocean." Equally remembered is his "prose poem." The first publication of this celebrated tribute first appeared, according to Paine's biography of Twain, in April 1889, when the author extemporaneously voiced it in an address at a dinner given to a victorious baseball team returning from a tour of the world by way of Hawaii. "He told of the curious island habits for his hearers' amusement, but at the close the poetry of his memories once more possessed him." Here is a fitting climax to any discussion of Mark Twain and Hawaii:

"No alien land in all the world has any deep strong charm for me but that one, no other land could so longingly and so beseechingly haunt me, sleeping and walking, through half a lifetime, as that one has done. Other things leave me, but it abides; other things change, but it remains the same. For me its balmy airs are always blowing, its summer seas flashing in the sun; the pulsing of its surfbeat is in my ear, I can see its garlanded crags, its leaping cascades, its plumy palms drowsing by the shore, its remote summits floating like islands above the cloud wrack; I can feel the spirit of its woodland solitudes, I can hear the splash of its brooks; in my nostrils still lives the breath of flowers that perished twenty years ago."

A. Grove Day

Chapter I

On a certain bright morning the Islands hove in sight, lying low on the lonely sea, and everybody climbed to the upper dock to look. After two thousand miles of watery solitude the vision was a welcome one. As we approached, the imposing promontory of Diamond Head rose up out of the ocean its rugged front softened by the hazy distance, and presently the details of the land began to make themselves manifest: first the line of beach; then the plumed coacoanut trees of the tropics; then cabins of the natives; then the white town of Honolulu, said to contain between twelve and fifteen thousand inhabitants spread over a dead level; with streets from twenty to thirty feet wide, solid and level as a floor, most of them straight as a line and few as crooked as a corkscrew.

The further I traveled through the town the better I liked it. Every step revealed a new contrast—disclosed something I was unaccustomed to. In place of the grand mud-colored brown fronts of San Francisco, I saw dwellings built of straw, adobies, and cream-colored pebble-and-shell-conglomerated coral, out into oblong blocks and laid in cement; also a great number of neat white cottages, with green window-shutters;

in place of front yards like billiard-tables with iron fences around them, I saw these homes surrounded by ample yards, thickly clad with green grass, and shaded by tall trees, through whose dense foliage the sun could scarcely penetrate; in place of the customary geranium, calla lily, etc., languishing in dust and general debility, I saw luxurious banks and thickets of flowers, fresh as a meadow after a rain, and glowing with the richest dyes; in place of the dingy horrors of San Francisco's pleasure grove, the "Willows," I saw huge-bodied, wide-spreading forest trees, with strange names and stranger appearance—trees that cast a shadowlike a thundercloud, and were able to stand alone without being tied to green poles; in place of gold fish, wiggling around in glass globes, assuming countless shades and degrees of distortion through the magnifying and diminishing qualities of their transparent prison houses, I saw cats—Tomcats, Mary Ann cats, long-tailed cats, bob-tailed cats, blind cats, one-eyed cats, wall-eyed cats, cross-eyed cats, gray cats, black cats, white cats, yellow cats, striped cats, spotted cats, tame cats, wild cats, singed cats, individual cats, groups of cats, platoons of cats, companies of cats, regiments of cats, armies of cats, multitudes of cats, millions of cats, and all of them sleek, fat, lazy and sound asleep.

I looked on a multitude of people, some white, in white coats, vests, pantaloons, even white cloth shoes, made snowy with chalk duly laid on every morning; but the majority of the people were almost as dark as negroes—women with comely features, fine black eyes, rounded forms, inclining to the voluptuous, clad in a single bright red or white garment that fell free and unconfined from shoulder to heel, long black hair falling loose, gypsy hats, encircled with wreaths of natural flowers of a brilliant carmine tint; plenty of dark men in various costumes, and some with nothing on but a battered stove-pipe hat tilted on the nose, and a very scant breech-clout;—certain smoke-dried children were clothed in nothing but sunshine—a very neat fitting and picturesque apparel indeed.

In place of roughs and rowdies staring and blackguarding on the corners, I saw long-haired, saddle-colored Sandwich Island maidens sitting on the ground in the shade of corner houses, gazing indolently at whatever or whoever happened along; instead of wretched cobble-stone pavements, I walked on a firm foundation of coral, built up from the bottom of the sea by the absurd but persevering insect of that name, with a light layer of lava and cinders overlying the coral, belched up out of fathomless perdition long ago through the seared and blackened crater that stands dead and harmless in the distance now; instead of cramped and crowded street-cars, I met dusky native women sweeping by, free as the wind, on fleet horses and astride, with gaudy riding-sashes, streaming like banners behind them; instead of the com-bined stenches of Chinadom and Brannan street slaughter-houses, I breathed the balmy fragrance of jessamine, olean-der, and the Pride of India; in place of the hurry and bustle and noisy confusion of San Francisco, I moved in the midst of a Summer calm as tranquil as dawn in the Garden of Eden; in place of the Golden City's skirting sand hills and the placid bay, I saw on the one side a frame-work of tall, precipitous mountains close at hand, clad in refreshing green, and deft by deep, cool, chasm-like valleys—and in front the grand sweep of the ocean: a brilliant, transparent green near the shore, bound and bordered by a long white line of foamy spray dashing against the reef, and further out the dead blue water of the deep sea, flecked with "white caps," axid in the far horizon a single, lonely sail—a mere accent-mark to emphasize a slumberous calm and a solitude that were with-out sound or limit. When the sun sunk down—the one intruder from other realms and persistent in suggestions of them—it was tranced luxury to sit in the perfumed air and forget that there was any world but these enchanted islands.

It was such ecstacy to dream, and dream—till you got a bite.

A scorpion bite. Then the first duty was to get up out of the grass and kill the scorpion; and the next to bathe the bitten place with alcohol or brandy; and the next to resolve to keep out of the grass in future. Then came an adjournment to the bedchamber and the pastime of writing up the day's journal with one hand and the destruction of mosquitoes with the other—a whole community of them at a slsp. Then, observing an enemy approaching,—a hairy tarantula on stilts—why not set the spittoon on him? It is done, and the projecting ends of his paws give a luminous idea of the magnitude of his reach. Then to bed and become a promenade for a centipede with forty-two legs on a side and every foot hot enough to burn a hole through a raw-hide. More soaking with alcohol, and a resolution to examine the bed before entering it, in future. Then wait, and suffer, till all the mosquitoes in the neighborhood have crawled in

under the bar, then slip out quickly, shut them in and sleep peacefully on the floor till morning. Meantime it is comforting to curse the tropics in occasional wakeful intervals.

We had an abundance of fruit in Honolulu, of course. Oranges, pine-apples, bananas, strawberries, lemons, limes, mangoes, guavas, melons, and a rare and curious luxury called the chirimoya, which is deliciousness itself. Then there is the tamarind. I thought tamarinds were made to eat, but that was probably not the idea. I ate several, and it seemed to me that they were rather sour that year. They pursed up my lips, till they resembled the stem-end of a tomato, and I had to take my sustenance through a quill for twenty-four hours. They sharpened my teeth till I could have shaved with them, and gave them a "wire edge" that I was afraid would stay; but a citizen said "no, it will come off when the enamel does"—which was comforting, at any rate. I found, afterward, that only strangers eat tamarinds—but they only eat them once.

Chapter II

In my diary of our third day in Honolulu, I find this:

I am probably the most sensitive man in Hawaii to-night—especially about sitting down in the presence of my betters. I have ridden fifteen or twenty miles on horse-back since 5 P.M. and to tell the honest truth, I have a delicacy about sitting down at all.

An excursion to Diamond Head and the King's Coacoanut Grove was planned to-day-time, 4:30 P.M.-the party to consist of half a dozen gentlemen and three ladies. They all started at the appointed hour except myself. I was at the Government prison, (with Captain Fish and another whaleship-skipper, Captain Phillips,) and got so interested in its examination that I did not notice how quickly the time was passing. Somebody remarked that it was twenty minutes past five o'clock, and that woke me up. It was a fortunate circumstance that Captain Phillips was; along with his "turn out," as he calls a top-buggy that Captain Cook brought here in 1778, and a horse that was here when Captain Cook came. Captain Phillips takes a just pride in his driving and in the speed of his horse, and to his passion for displaying them I owe it that we were only sixteen minutes coming from the prison to the American Hotel—a distance which has been estimated to be over half a mile. But it took some fearful driving. The Captain's whip came down fast, and the blows started so much dust out of the horse's hide that during the last half of the journey we rode through an impenetrable fog, and ran by a pocket compass in the hands of Captain Fish, a whaler of twenty-six years experience, who sat there through the perilous voyage as self-possesed as if he had been on the euchre-deck of his own ship, and calmly said, "Port your helm—port," from time to time, and "Hold her a little free—steady—so-o," and "Luff—hard down to starboard!" and never once lost his presence of mind or betrayed the least anxiety by voice or manner. When we came to anchor at last, and Captain Phillips looked at his watch and said, "Sixteen minutes—I told you it was in her! that's over three miles an hour!" I could see he felt entitled to a compliment, and so I said I had never seen lightning go like that horse. And I never had.

The landlord of the American said the party had been gone nearly an hour, but that he could give me my choice of several horses that could overtake them. I said, never mind— I preferred a safe horse to a fast one—I would like to have an excessively gentle horse—a horse with no spirit whatever— a lame one, if he had such a thing. Inside of five minutes I was mounted, and perfectly satisfied with my outfit. I had no time to label him "This is a horse," and so if the public took him for a sheep I cannot help it. I was satisfied, and that was the main thing. I could see that he had as many fine points as any man's horse, and so I hung my hat on one of them, behind the saddle, and swabbed the perspiration from my face and started. I named him after this island, "Oahu" (pronounced O-waw-hee). The first gate he came to he started in; I had neither whip nor spur, and so I simply argued the case with him. He resisted argument, but ultimately yielded to insult and abuse. He backed out of that gate and steered for another one on the other side of the street. I triumphed by my former process. Within the next six hundred yards he crossed the street fourteen times and attempted thirteen gates, and in the meantime the tropical sun was beating down and threatening to cave the top of my head in, and I was literally dripping with perspiration. He abandoned the gate business after that and went along peaceably enough, but absorbed in meditation. I noticed this latter circumstance, and it soon began to fill me with apprehension. I said to myself, this creature is planning some new outrage, some fresh deviltry or other—no horse ever thought over a subject so profoundly as this one is doing just for nothing. The more this thing preyed upon my mind the more uneasy I became, until the suspense became almost unbearable and I dismounted to see if there was anything wild in his eye—for I had heard that the eye of this noblest of our domestic animals is very expressive. I cannot describe what a load of anxiety was lifted from my mind when I found that he was only asleep. I woke him up and started him into a faster walk, and then the villainy of his nature came out again. He tried to climb over a stone wall, five or six feet high. I saw that I must apply force to this horse, and that I might as well begin first as last. I plucked a stout switch from a tamarind tree, and the moment he saw it, he surrendered. He broke into a convulsive sort of a canter, which had three short steps in it and one long one, and reminded me alternately of the clattering shake of the great earthquake, and the sweeping plunging of the Ajax* in a storm.

And now there can be no fitter occasion than the present to pronounce a left-handed blessing upon the man who invented the American saddle. There is no seat to speak of about it—one might as well sit in a shovel—and the stirrups are nothing but an ornamental nuisance. If I were to write

* The boat Twain sailed on to Hawaii.—editor.

down here all the abuse I expended on those stirrups, it would make a large book, even without pictures. Sometimes I got one foot so far through, that the stirrup partook of the nature of an anklet; sometimes both feet were through, and I was handcuffed by the legs; and sometimes my feet got clear out and left the stirrups wildly dangling about my shins. Even when I was in proper position and carefully balanced upon the balls of my feet, there was no comfort in it, on account of my nervous dread that they were going to slip one way or the other in a moment. But the subject is too exasperating to write about.

A mile and a half from town, I come to a grove of tall cocoanut trees, with clean, branchless stems reaching straight up sixty or seventy feet and topped with a spray of green foliage sheltering

clusters of cocoanuts—not more picturesque than a forest of collossal ragged parasols, with bunches of magnified grapes under them, would be. I once heard a grouty northern invalid say that a cocoanut tree might be poetical, possibly it was; but it looked like a feather-duster struck by lightning. I think that describes it better than a picture—and yet, without any question, there is something fascinating about a cocoa-nut tree—and graceful, too.

About a dozen cottages, some frame and the others of native grass, nestled sleepily in the shade here and there. The grass cabins are of a grayish color, are shaped much like our own cottages, only with higher and steeper roofs usually, and are made of some kind of weed strongly bound together in bundles. The roofs are very thick, and so are the walls; the latter have square holes in them for windows. At a little distance these cabins have a furry appearance, as if they might be made of bear skins. They are very cool and pleasant inside. The King's flag was flying from the roof of one of the cottages, and His Majesty was probably within. He owns the whole concern thereabouts, and passes his time there frequently, on sultry days "laying off." The spot is called "The King's Grove."

Near by is an interesting ruin—the meagre remains of an ancient heathen temple—a place where human sacrifices were offered up in those old bygone days when the simple child of nature, yielding momentarily to sin when sorely tempted, acknowledged his error when calm reflection had shown it him, and came forward with noble frankness and offered up his grandmother as an atoning sacrifice—in those old days when the luckless sinner could keep on cleansing his conscience and achieving periodical happiness as long as his relations held out; long, long before the missionaries braved a thousand privations to come and make them permanently miserable by telling them how beautiful and how blissful a place heaven is, and how nearly impossible it is to get there; and showed the poor native how dreary a place perdition is and what unnecessarily liberal facilities there are for going to it; showed him how, in his ignorance he had gone and fooled away all his kinfolks to no purpose; showed him what rapture it is to work all day long for fifty cents to buy food for next day with, as compared with fishing for pastime and lolling in the shade through eternal Summer, and eating of the bounty that nobody labored to provide but Nature. How sad it is to think of the multitudes who have gone to their graves in this beautiful island and never knew there was a hell!

This ancient temple was built of rough blocks of lava, and was simply a roofless inclosure a hundred and thirty feet long and seventy wide—nothing but naked walls, very thick, but not much higher than a man's head. They will last for ages no doubt, if left unmolested. Its three altars and other sacred appurtenances have crumbled and passed away years ago. It is said that in the old times thousands of human beings were slaughtered here, in the presence of naked and howling savages. If these mute stones could speak, what tales they could tell, what pictures they could describe, of fettered victims writhing under the knife; of massed forms straining forward out of the gloom, with ferocious faces lit up by the sacrificial fires; of the background of ghostly trees; of the dark pyramid of Diamond Head standing sentinel over the uncanny scene, and the peaceful moon looking down upon it through rifts in the cloud-rack!

When Kamehameha (pronounced Ka-may-ha-may-ah) the Great—who was a sort of a Napoleon in military genius and uniform success—invaded this island of Oahu three quarters of a century ago, and exterminated the army sent to oppose him, and took full and final possession of the country, he searched out the dead body of the King of Oahu, and those of the principal chiefs, and impaled their heads on the walls of this temple.

Those were savage times when this old slaughter-house was in its prime. The King and the chiefs ruled the common herd with a rod of iron; made them gather all the provisions the masters needed; build all the houses and temples; stand all the expenses, of whatever kind; take kicks and cuffs for thanks; drag out lives well flavored with misery, and then suffer death for trifling offences or yield up their lives on the sacrificial altars to purchase favors from the gods for their hard rulers. The missionaries have clothed them, educated them, broken up the tyrannous authority of their chiefs, and given them freedom and the right to enjoy whatever their hands and brains produce with equal laws for all, and punishment for all alike who transgress them. The contrast is so strong—the benefit conferred upon this people by the missionaries is so prominent, so palpable and so unquestionable, that the frankest compliment I can pay them, and the best, is simply to point to the condition of the Sandwich Islanders of Captain Cook's time, and their condition today. Their work speaks for itself.

Chapter III

B y and by, after a rugged climb, we halted on the summit of a hill which commanded a far-reaching view. The moon rose and flooded mountain and valley and ocean with a mellow radiance, and out of the shadows of the foliage the distant lights of Honolulu glinted like an encampment of fireflies. The air was heavy with the fragrance of flowers. The halt was brief.—Gayly laughing and talking, the party galloped on, and I clung to the pommel and cantered after. Presently we came to a place where no grass grew—a wide expanse of deep sand. They said it was an old battle ground. All around everywhere, not three feet apart, the bleached bones of men gleamed white in the moonlight. We picked up a lot of them for mementoes. I got quite a number of arm bones and leg bones—of great chiefs, may be, who had fought savagely in that fearful battle in the old days, when blood flowed like wine where we now stood.—and wore the choicest of them out on Oahu afterward, trying to make him go. All sorts of bones could be found except skulls; but a citizen said, irreverently, that there had been an unusual number of "skull-hunters" there lately"—a species of sports-men I had never heard of before.

Nothing whatever is known about this place—its story is a secret that will never be revealed. The oldest natives make no pretense of being possessed of its history. They say these bones were here when they were children. They were here when their grandfathers were children—but how they came here, they can only conjecture. Many people believe this spot to be an ancient battle-ground, and it is usual to call it so; and they believe that these skeletons have lain for ages just where their proprietors fell in the great fight. Other people believe that Kamehameha I. fought his first battle here. On this point, I have heard a story, which may have been taken from one of the numerous books which have been written concerning these islands—I do not know where the narrator got it. He said that when Kamehameha (who was at first merely a subordinate chief on the island of Hawaii), landed here, he brought a large army with him, and encamped at Waikiki. The Oahuans marched against him, and so confident were they of success that they readily acceded to a demand of their priests that they should draw a line where these bones now lie, and take an oath that, if forced to retreat at all, they would never retreat beyond this boundary. The priests told them that death and everlasting punishment would overtake any who violated the oath, and the march was resumed. Kamehameha drove them back step by step; the priests fought in the front rank and exhorted them both by voice and inspiriting example to remember their oath—to die, if need be, but never cross the fatal line. The struggle was manfully maintained, but at last the chief priest fell, pierced to the heart with a spear, and the unlucky omen fell like a blight upon the brave souls at his back; with a triumphant shout the invaders pressed forward-the line was crossed—the offended gods deserted the despairing army, and, accepting the doom their perjury had brought upon them, they broke and fled over the plain where Honolulu stands now—up the beautiful Nuuanu Valley—paused a moment, hemmed in by precipitous mountains on either hand and the frightful precipice of the Pari in front, and then were driven over—a sheer plunge of six hundred feet!

The story is pretty enough, but Mr. Jarves' excellent history says the Oahuans were entrenched in Nuuanu Valley; that Kamehameha ousted them, routed them, pursued them up the valley and drove them over the precipice. He makes no mention of our bone-yard at all in his book.

Impressed by the profound silence and repose that rested over the beautiful landscape, and being, as usual, in the rear, I gave voice to my thoughts. I said:

"What a picture is here slumbering in the solemn glory of the moon! How strong the rugged outlines of the dead volcano stand out against the clear sky! What a snowy fringe marks the bursting of the surf over the long, curved reef! How calmly the dim city sleeps yonder in the plain! How soft the shadows lie upon the stately mountains that border the dream-haunted Mauoa Valley! What a grand pyramid of billowy clouds towers above the storied Pari! How the grim warriors of the past seem flocking in ghostly squadrons to their ancient battlefield again—how the wails of the dying well up from the—"

At this point the horse called Oahu sat down in the sand. Sat down to listen, I suppose. Never mind what he heard, I stopped apostrophising and convinced him that I was not a man to allow contempt of Court on the part of a horse. I broke the back-bone of a Chief over his rump and set out to join the cavalcade again.

Very considerably fagged out we arrived in town at 9 o'clock at night, myself in the lead—for when my horse finally came to understand that he was homeward bound and hadn't far to go, he turned his attention strictly to business.

This is a good time to drop in a paragraph of information. There is no regular livery stable in Honolulu, or, indeed, in any part of the kingdom of Hawaii; therefore unless you are acquainted with wealthy residents (who all have good horses), you must hire animals of the wretchedest description from the Kanakas. (i.e. natives.) Any horse you hire, even though it be from a white man, is not often of much account, because it will be brought in for you from some ranch, and has necessarily been leading a hard life. If the Kanakas who have been caring for him (inveterate riders they are) have not ridden him half to death every day themselves, you can depend upon it they have been doing the same thing by proxy, by clandestinely hiring him out. At least, so I am informed. The result is, that no horse has a chance to eat, drink, rest, recuperate, or look well or feel well, and so strangers go about the Islands mounted as I was to-day.

In hiring a horse from a Kanaka, you must have all your eyes about you, because you can rest satisfied that you are dealing with a shrewd unprincipled rascal. You may leave your door open and your trunk unlocked as long as you please, and he will not meddle with your property; he has no important vices and no inclination to commit robbery on a large scale; but if he can get ahead of you in the horse business, he will take a genuine delight in doing it. This trait is characteristic of horse jockeys, the world over, is it not? He will overcharge you if he can; he will hire you a fine-looking horse at night (anybody's—may be the King's, if the royal steed be in convenient view), and bring you the mate to my Oahu in the morning, and contend that it is the same animal. If you make trouble, he will get out by saying it was not himself who made the bargain with you, but his brother, "who went out in the country this morning." They have always got a "brother" to shift the responsibility upon. A victim said to one of these fellows one day:

"But I know I hired the horse of you, because I noticed that scar on your cheek."

The reply was not bad: "Oh, yes—yes—my brother all same—we twins!"

A friend of mine, J. Smith, hired a horse yesterday, the Kanaka warranting him to be in excellent condition. Smith had a saddle and blanket of his own, and he ordered the Kanaka to put these on the horse. The Kanaka protested that he was perfectly willing to trust the gentleman with the saddle that was already on the animal, but Smith refused to use it. The change was made; then Smith noticed that the Kanaka had only changed the saddles, and had left the original blanket on the horse; he said he forgot to change the blankets, and so, to cut the bother short, Smith mounted and rode away. The horse went lame a mile from town, and afterward got to cutting up some extraordinary capers. Smith got down and took off the saddle, but the blanket stuck fast to the horse—glued to a procession of raw places. The Kanaka's mysterious conduct stood explained.

Another friend of mine bought a pretty good horse from a native, a day or two ago, after a tolerably thorough examination of the animal. He discovered today that the horse was as blind as a bat, in one eye. He meant to have examined that eye, and came home with a general notion that he had done it; but he remembers now that every time he made the attempt his attention was called to something else by his victimizer.

One more instance, and then I will pas to something else. I am informed that when a certain Mr. L., a visiting stranger, was here, he bought a pair of very respectable-looking match horses from a native. They were in a little stable with a partition through the middle of it—one horse in each apartment. Mr. L. examined one of them critically through a window (the Kanaka's "brother" having gone to the country with the key), and then went around the house and examined the other through a window on the other side. He said it was the neatest match he had ever seen, and paid for the horses on the spot. Whereupon the Kanaka departed to join his brother in the country. The fellow had shamefully swindled L. There was only one "match" horse, and he had examined his starboard side through one window and his port side through another! I decline to believe this story, but I give it because it is worth something as a fanciful illustration of a fixed fact—namely, that the Kanaka horse-jockey is fertile in invention and elastic in conscience.

You can buy a pretty good horse for forty or fifty dollars, and a good enough horse for all practical purposes for two dollars and a half. I estimate "Oahu" to be worth somewhere in the neighborhood of thirty-five cents. A good deal better animal than he is was sold here day before yesterday for a dollar and seventy-five cents, and sold again to-day for two dollars and twenty-five cents; Williams bought a handsome and lively little pony yesterday for ten dollars; and about the best common horse on the island (and he is a really good one) sold yesterday, with Mexican saddle and bridle, for seventy dollars—a horse which is well and widely known, and greatly respected for his speed, good disposition and everlasting bottom. You give your horse a little grain once a day; it comes from San Francisco, and is worth about two cents a pound; and you give him as much hay as he wants; it is cut and brought to the market by natives, and is not very good it is baled into long, round bundles, about the size of a large man; one of them is stuck by the middle on each end of a six-foot pole, and the Kanaka shoulders the pole and walks about the streets between the upright bales in search of customers. These hay bales, thus carried, have a general resemblance to a colonial capital H.

The hay-bundles cost twenty-five cents apiece, and one

will last a horse about a day. You can get a horse for a song, a week's hay for another song, and you can turn your animal loose among the luxuriant grass in your neighbor's broad front yard without a song at all—you do it at midnight, and stable the beast again before morning. You have been at no expense thus far, but when you come to buy a saddle and bridle they will cost you from twenty to thirty-five dollars. You can hire a horse, saddle and bridle at from seven to ten dollars a week, and the owner will take care of them at his own expense.

It is time to close this day's record—bed time. As I prepare for sleep, a rich voice rises out of the still night, and, far as this ocean rock is toward the ends of the earth, I recognize a familiar home air. But the words seem somewhat out of joint:

"Waikiki lantoni oe Kaa hooly hooly wawhoo."

Translated, that means "When we were marching through Georgia."

Chapter IV

Passing through the market place we saw that feature of Honolulu under its most favorable auspices—that is, in the full glory of Saturday afternoon, which is a festive day with the natives. The native girls by twos and threes and parties of a dozen, and sometimes in whole platoons and companies, went sauntering up and down the neighboring streets astride of fleet but homely horses, and with their gaudy riding habits streaming like banners behind them. Such a troop of free and easy riders, in their natural home, the saddle, makes a gay and graceful spectacle. The riding habit I speak of is simply a long, broad scarf, like a tavern table cloth brilliantly colored, wrapped around the loins once, then apparently passed between the limbs and each end thrown backward over the same, and floating and flapping behind on both sides beyond the horse's tail like a couple of fancy flags; then, slipping the stirrup-irons between her toes, the girl throws her chest forward, sits up like a Major General and goes sweeping by like the wind.

The girls put on all the finery they can on Saturday afternoon—fine black silk robes; flowing red ones that nearly put your eyes out; others as white as snow; still others that discount the rainbow; and they wear their hair in nets, and trim their jaunty hats with fresh flowers, and encircle their dusky throats with home-made necklaces of the brilliant vermillion-tinted blossom of the *ohia*; and they fill the markets and the adjacent streets with their bright presences, and smell like a rag factory on fire with their offensive cocoanut oil.

Occasionally you see s heathen from the sunny isles away down in the South Seas, with his face and neck tatooed till he looks like the customary mendicant from Washoe who has been blown up in a mine. Some are tattooed a dead blue color down to the upper lip—masked, as it were—leaving the natural light yellow skin of Micronesia unstained from thence down; some with broad marks drawn down from hair to neck, on both sides of the face, and a strip of the original yellow skin, two inches wide, down the center—a gridiron with a spoke broken out; and some with the entire face discolored with the popular mortification tint, relieved only by one or two thin, wavy threads of natural yellow running across the face from ear to ear, and eyes twinkling out of this darkness, from under shadowing hat-brims, like stars in the dark of the moon.

Moving among the stirring crowds, you come to the poi merchants, squatting in the shade on their hams, in true native fashion, and surrounded by purchasers. (The Sandwich Islanders always squat on their hams, and who knows but they may be the old original "ham sandwiches?" The thought is pregnant with interest.) The poi looks like common flour paste, and is kept in large bowls formed of a species of gourd, and capable of holding from one to three or four gallons. Poi is the chief article of food among the natives, and is prepared from the *taro* plant. The taro root looks like a thick, or, if you please, a corpulent sweet potato, in shape, but is of a light purple color when boiled. When boiled it answers as a

passable substitute for bread. The buck Kanakas bake it
under ground, then mash it up well with a heavy lava pestle,
mix water with it until it becomes a paste, set it aside and let
it ferment, and then it is poi—and an unseductive mixture it
is, almost tasteless before it ferments and too sour for a
luxury afterward. But nothing is more nutritious. When
solely used, however, it produces acrid humors, a fact which
sufficiently accounts for the humorous character of the
Kanakas. I think there must be as much of a knack in
handling poi as there is in eating with chopsticks. The
forefinger is thrust into the mess and stirred quickly round
several times and drawn as quickly out, thickly coated, just
as if it were poulticed; the head is thrown back, the finger
inserted in the mouth and the delicacy stripped off and
swallowed-the eye closing gently, meanwhile, in a languid
sort of ecstasy. Many a different finger goes into the same
bowl and many a different kind of dirt and shade and quality
of flavor is added to the virtues of its contents.

Around a small shanty was collected a crowd of natives
buying the *awa* root. It is said that but for the use of this root
the destruction of the people in former times by certain
imported diseases would have been far greater than it was,
and by others it is said that this is merely a fancy. All agree
that poi will rejuvenate a man who is used up and his vitality
almost annihilated by hard drinking, and that in some kinds
of diseases it will restore health after all medicines have
failed; but all are not willing to allow to the *awa* the virtues
claimed for it. The natives manufacture an intoxicating
drink from it which is fearful in its effects when persistently
indulged in. It covers the body with dry, white scales, in-
flames the eyes, and causes premature decrepitude. Although
the man before whose establishment we stopped has to pay a
Government license of eight hundred dollars a year for the
exclusive right to sell awa root, it is said that he makes a

small fortune every twelve-month; while saloon keepers, who pay a thousand dollars a year for the privilege of retailing whiskey, etc., only make a bare living.

We found the fish market crowded; for the native is very fond of fish, and *eats the article raw and alive!* Let us change the subject.

In old times here Saturday was a grand gala day indeed. All the native population of the town forsook their labors, and those of the surrounding country journeyed to the city. Then the white folks had to stay indoors, for every street was so packed with charging cavaliers and cavalieresses that it was next to impossible to thread one's way through the cavalcades without getting crippled.

At night they feasted and the girls danced the lascivious *hula hula* dance that is said to exhibit the very perfection of educated motion of limb and arm, hand, head and body, and the exactest uniformity of movement and accuracy of "time." It was performed by a circle of girls with no raiment on them to speak of, who went through an infinite variety of motions and figures without prompting, and yet so true was their "time," and in such perfect concert did they move that when they were placed in a straight line, hands, arms, bodies, limbs and heads waved, swayed, gesticulated, bowed, stooped, whirled, squirmed, twisted and undulated as if they were part and parcel of a single individual; and it was difficult to believe they were not moved in a body by some exquisite piece of mechanism.

Of late years, however, Saturday has lost most of its quondam gala features. This weekly stampede of the natives interfered too much with labor and the interests of the white folks, and by sticking in a law here, and preaching a sermon there, and by various other means, they gradually broke it up. The demoralizing *hula hula* forbidden to be performed, save at night, with closed doors, in presence of few spectators, and only by permission duly procured from the authorities and the payment of ten dollars for the same. There are few girls now-a-days able to dance this ancient national dance in the highest perfection of the art.

The missionaries have christianized and educated all the natives. They all belong to the Church, and there is not one of them, above the age of eight years, but can read and write with facility in the native tongue. It is the most universally educated race of people outside of China. They have any quantity of books, printed in the Kanaka language, and all the natives are fond of reading. They are inveterate church-goers—nothing can keep them away. All this ameliorating cultivation has at last built up in the native women a profound respect for chastity—in other people. Perhaps that is enough to say on that head. The national sin will die out when the race does, but perhaps not earlier.—But doubtless this purifying is not far off, when we reflect that contact with civilization and the whites has reduced the native population from *four hundred thousand* (Captain Cook's estimate,) to *fifty-five thousand* in something over eighty years!

Society is a queer medley in this notable missionary, whaling and governmental centre. If you get into conversation with a stranger and experience that natural desire to know what sort of ground you are treading on by finding out what manner of man your stranger is, strike out boldly and address him as "Captain." Watch him narrowly, and if you see by his countenance that you are on the wrong tack, ask him where he preaches. It is a safe bet that he is either a missionary or captain of a whaler. I am now personally acquainted with seventy-two captains and ninety-six missionaries. The captains and ministers form one-half of the population; the third fourth is composed of common Kanakas and mercantile foreigners and their families, and the final fourth is made up of high officers of the Hawaiian

Government. And there are just about cats enough for three apiece all around.

A solemn stranger met me in the suburbs the other day, and said:

"Good morning, your reverence. Preach in the stone church yonder, no doubt?"

"No, I don't. I'm not a preacher."

"Really, I beg your pardon, Captain. I trust you had a good season. How much oil"— "Oil? What do you take me for? I'm not a whaler."

"Oh, I beg a thousand pardons, your Excellency. Major General in the household troops, no doubt? Minister of the Interior, likely? Secretary of war? First Gentleman of the Bed-chamber? Commissioner of the Royal"—

"Stuff! I'm no official. I'm not connected in any way with the Government."

"Bless my life! Then, who the mischief are you? what the mischief are you? and how the mischief did you get here, and where in thunder did you come from? "

"I'm only a private personage—an unassuming stranger—lately arrived from America."

"No? Not a missionary! Not a whaler! not a member of His Majesty's Government! not even Secretary of the Navy! Ah, Heaven! it is too blissful to be true; alas, I do but dream. And yet that noble, honest countenance—those oblique, ingenuous eyes—that massive head, incapable of—of—anything; your hand; give me your hand, bright waif. Excuse these tears. For sixteen weary years I have yearned for a moment like this, and"—

Here his feelings were too much for him, and he swooned away. I pitied this poor creature from the bottom of my heart. I was deeply moved. I shed a few tears on him and kissed him for his mother. I then took what small change he had and "shoved."

Chapter V

I still quote from my journal:

I found the national Legislature to consist of half a dozen white men and some thirty or forty natives. It was a dark assemblage. The nobles and Ministers (about a dozen of them altogether) occupied the extreme left of the hall, with David Kalakaua (the King's Chamberlain) and Prince William at the head. The President of the Assembly, His Royal Highness M. Kekuanaoa,* and the Vice President (the latter a white man') sat in the pulpit, if I may so term it.

The President is the King's father. He is an erect, strongly built, massive featured, white-haired, tawny old gentleman of eighty years of age or thereabouts. He was simply but well dressed, in a blue cloth coat and white vest, and white pantaloons, without spot, dust or blemish upon them. He bears himself with a calm, stately dignity, and is a man of noble presence. He was a young man and a distinguished warrior under that terrific fighter, Kamehameha I., more than half a century ago. A knowledge of his career suggested some such thought as this: "This man, naked as the day he was born, and war-club and spear in hand, has charged at the head of a horde of savages against other hordes of savages

*Since dead.

more than a generation and a half ago, and reveled in slaughter and carnage; has worshipped wooden images on his devout knees; has seen hundreds of his race offered up in heathen temples as sacrifices to wooden idols, at a time when no missionary's foot had ever pressed this soil, and he had never heard of the white man's God; has believed his enemy could secretly pray him to death; has seen the day, in his childhood, when it was a crime punishable by death for a man to eat with his wife, or for a plebeian to let his shadow fall upon the King—and now look at him; an educated Christian; neatly and handsomely dressed; a high-minded, elegant gentleman; a traveler, in some degree, and one who has been the honored guest of royalty in Europe; a man practiced in holding the reins of an enlightened government, and well versed in the polities of his country and in general, practical information. Look at him, sitting there presiding over the deliberations of a legislative body, among whom are white men—a grave, dignified, statesmanlike personage, and as seemingly natural and fitted to the place as if he had been born in it and had never been out of it in his life time. How the experiences of this old man's eventful life shame the cheap inventions of romance!"

Kekuanaoa is not of the blood royal. He derives his princely rank from his wife, who was a daughter of Kamehameha the Great. Under other monarchies the male line takes precedence of the female in tracing genealogies, but here the opposite is the case—the female line takes precedence. Their reason for this is exceedingly sensible, and I recommend it to the aristocracy of Europe: They say it is easy to know who a man's mother was, but, etc., etc. The christianizing of the natives has hardly even weakened some of their barbarian superstitions, much less destroyed them. I have just referred to one of these. It is still a popular belief that if your enemy can get hold of any article belonging to you he can get down on his knees over it and pray you to death. Therefore many a native gives up and dies merely because he imagines that some enemy is putting him through a course of damaging prayer. This praying an individual to death seems absurd enough at a first glance, but then when we call to mind some of the pulpit efforts of certain of our own ministers the thing looks plausible.

In former times, among the Islanders, not only a plurality of wives was customary, but a plurality of husbands likewise. Some native women of noble rank had as many as six husbands. A woman thus supplied did not reside with all her husbands at once, but lived several months with each in turn. An understood sign hung at her door during these months. When the sign was taken down, it meant "NEXT."

In those days woman was rigidly taught to "know her place." Her place was to do all the work, take all the cuffs, provide all the food, and content herself with what was left after her lord had finished his dinner. She was not only forbidden, by ancient law, and under penalty of death, to eat with her husband or enter a canoe, but was debarred, under the same penalty, from eating bananas, pine-apples, oranges and other choice fruits at any time or in any place. She had to confine herself pretty strictly to "poi" and hard work. These poor ignorant heathen seem to have had a sort of groping idea of what came of woman eating fruit in the garden of Eden, and they did not choose to take any more chances. But the missionaries broke up this satisfactory arrangement of things. They liberated woman and made her the equal of man.

The natives had a romantic fashion of burying some of their children alive when the family became larger than necessary. The missionaries interfered in this matter too, and stopped it.

To this day the natives are able to lie down and die

whenever they want to, whether there is anything the matter with them or not. If a Kanaka takes a notion to die, that is the end of him; nobody can persuade him to hold on; all the doctors in the world could not save him.

A luxury which they enjoy more than anything else, is a large funeral. If a person wants to get rid of a troublesome native, it is only necessary to promise him a fine funeral and name the hour and he will be on hand to the minute—at least his remains will.

All the natives are Christians, now, but many of them still desert to the Great Shark God for temporary succor in time of trouble. An irruption of the great volcano of Kilauea, or an earthquake, always brings a deal of latent loyalty to the Great Shark God to the surface. It is common report that the King, educated, cultivated and refined Christian gentleman as he undoubtedly is, still turns to the idols of his fathers for help when disaster threatens. A planter caught a shark, and one of his christianized natives testified his emancipation from the thrall of ancient superstition by assisting to dissect the shark after a fashion forbidden by his abandoned creed. But remorse shortly began to torture him. He grew moody and sought solitude; brooded over his sin, refused food, and finally said he must die and ought to die, for he had sinned against the Great Shark God and could never know peace any more. He was proof against persuasion and ridicule, and in the course of a day or two took to his bed and died, although he showed no symptom of disease. His young daughter followed his lead and suffered a like fate within the week. Superstition is ingrained in the native blood and bone and it is only natural that it should crop out in time of distress. Wherever one goes in the Islands, he will find small piles of stones by the wayside, covered with leafy offerings, placed there by the natives to appease evil spirits or honor local deities belonging to the mythology of former days.

In the rural districts of any of the Islands, the traveler hourly comes upon parties of dusky maidens bathing in the streams or in the sea without any clothing on and exhibiting no very intemperate zeal in the matter of hiding their nakedness. When the missionaries first took up their residence in Honolulu, the native women would pay their families frequent friendly visits, day by day, not even clothed with a blush. It was found a hard matter to convince them that this was rather indelicate. Finally the missionaries provided them with long, loose calico robes, and that ended the difficulty— for the women would troop through the town, stark naked, with their robes folded under their arms, march to the missionary houses and then proceed to dress!—The natives soon manifested a strong proclivity for clothing, but it was shortly apparent that they only wanted it for grandeur. The missionaries imported a quantity of hats, bonnets, and other male and female wearing apparel, instituted a general distribution, and begged the people not to come to church naked, next Sunday, as usual. And they did not; but the national spirit of unselfishness led them to divide up with neighbors who were not at the distribution, and next Sabbath the poor preachers could hardly keep countenance before their vast congregations. In the midst of the reading of a hymn a brown, stately dame would sweep up the aisle with a world of airs, with nothing in the world on but a "stovepipe" hat and a pair of cheap gloves; another dame would follow, tricked out in a man's shirt, and nothing else; another one would enter with a flourish, with simply the sleeves of a bright calico dress tied around her waist and the rest of the garment dragging behind like a peacock's tail off duty; a stately "buck" Kanaka would stalk in with a woman's bonnet on, wrong side before—only this, and nothing more; after him would stride his fellow, with the legs of a pair of pantaloons tied around his neck, the rest of his person untrammeled; in his rear would come another gentleman simply gotten up in a fiery neck-tie and a striped vest. The poor creatures were beaming with complacency and wholly unconscious of any absurdity in their appearance. They gazed at each other with happy admiration, and it was plain to see that the young girls were taking note of what each other had on, as naturally as if they had always lived in a land of Bibles and knew what churches were made for; here was the evidence of a dawning civilization. The spectacle which the congregation presented was so extraordinary and withal so moving, that the missionaries found it difficult to keep to the text and go on with the services; and by and by when the simple children of the sun began a general swapping of garments in open meeting and produced some irresistibly grotesque effects in the course of re-dressing, there was nothing for it but to cut the thing short with the benediction and dismiss the fantastic assemblage.

In our country, children play "keep house;" and in the same high-sounding but miniature way the grown folk here, with the poor little material of slender territory and meagre population, play "empire." There is his royal Majesty the King, with a New York detective's income of thirty or thirty-five thousand dollars a year from the "royal civil list" and the "royal domain." He lives in a two-story frame "palace."

And there is the "royal family"—the customary hive of royal brothers, sisters, cousins and other noble drones and vagrants usual to monarchy,—all with a spoon in the national pap-dish, and all bearing such titles as his or her Royal Highness the Prince or Princess So-and-so. Few of them can carry their royal splendors far enough to ride in carriages, however; they sport the economical Kanaka horse or "hoof it"* with the plebeians.

Then there is his Excellency the "royal Chamberlain"—a

*Missionary phrase.

sinecure, for his majesty dresses himself with his own hands, except when he is ruralizing at Waikiki and then he requires no dressing.

Next we have His Excellency the Commander-in-chief of the Household Troops, whose forces consist of about the number of soldiers usually placed under a corporal in other lands.

Next comes the royal Steward and the Grand Equerry in Waiting—high dignitaries with modest salaries and little to do.

Then we have his Excellency the First Gentleman of the Bed-chamber—an office as easy as it is magnificent.

Next we come to his Excellency the Prime Minister, a renegade American from New Hampshire, all jaw, vanity, bombast and ignorance, a lawyer of "shyster " calibre, a fraud by nature, a humble worshiper of the sceptre above him, a reptile never tired of sneering at the land of his birth or glorifying the tenure kingdom that has adopted him—salary, $4,000 a year, vast consequence, and no perquisites.

Then we have his Excellency the Imperial Minister of Finance, who handles a million dollars of public money a year, sends in his annual "budget " with great ceremony, talks prodigiously of "finance," suggests imposing schemes for paying off the "national debt" (of $150,000,) and does it all for $4,000 a year and unimaginable glory. Next we have his Excellency the Minister of War, who holds sway over the royal armies—they consist of two hundred and thirty uniformed Kanakas, mostly Brigadier Generals, and if the country ever gets into trouble with a foreign power we shall probably hear from them. I knew an American whose copperplate visiting card bore this impressive legend: "Lieutenant-Colonel in the Royal Infantry." To say that he was proud of this distinction is stating it but tamely. The Minister of War has also in his charge some venerable swivels on Punch-

Bowl Hill wherewith royal salutes are fired when foreign vessels of war enter the port.

Next comes his Excellency the Minister of the Navy—a nabob who rules the "royal fleet," (a steam-tug and a sixty-ton schooner.)

And next comes his Grace the Lord Bishop of Honolulu, the chief dignitary of the "Established Church"—for when the American Presbyterian missionaries had completed the reduction of the nation to a compact condition of Christianity, native royalty stepped in and erected the grand dignity of an "Established (Episcopal) Church" over it, and imported a cheap ready-made Bishop from England to take charge. The chagrin of the missionaries has never been comprehensively expressed, to this day, profanity not being admissible.

Next comes his Excellency the Minister of Public Instruction.

Next, their Excellencies the Governors of Oahu, Hawaii, etc., and after them a string of High Sheriffs and other small fry too numerous for computation.

Then there are their Excellencies the Envoy Extraordinary and Minister Plenipotentiary of his Imperial Majesty the Emperor of the French; her British Majesty's Minister; the Minister Resident, of the United States; and some six or eight representatives of other foreign nations, all with sounding titles, imposing dignity and prodigious but economical state.

Imagine all this grandeur in a play-house "kingdom" whose population falls absolutely short of sixty thousand souls!

The people are so accustomed to nine-jointed titles and colossal magnates that a foreign prince makes very little more stir in Honolulu than a Western Congressman does in New York.

And let it be borne in mind that there is a strictly defined "court costume" of so "stunning" a nature that it would make the clown in a circus look tame and commonplace by comparison; and each Hawaiian official dignitary has a gorgeous vari-colored, gold-laced uniform peculiar to his office—no two of them are alike, and it is hard to tell which one is the "loudest." The King had a "drawing-room" at stated intervals, like other monarchs, and when these varied uniforms congregate there weak-eyed people have to contemplate the spectacle through smoked glass. Is there not a gratifying contrast between this latter-day exhibition and the one the ancestors of some of these magnates afforded the missionaries the Sunday after the old-time distribution of clothing? Behold what religion and civilization have wrought!

Chapter VI

While I was in Honolulu I witnessed the ceremonious funeral of the King's sister, her Royal Highness the Princess Victoria. According to the royal custom, the remains had lain in state at the palace thirty days, watched day and night by a guard of honor. And during all that time a great multitude of natives from the several islands had kept the palace grounds well crowded and had made the place a pandemonium every night with their howlings and wailings, beating of tom-toms and dancing of the (at other times) forbidden "hula hula" by half-clad maidens to the music of songs of questionable decency chanted in honor of the deceased. The printed programme of the funeral procession interested me at the time; and after what I have just said of Hawaiian grandiloquence in the matter of "playing empire," I am persuaded that a perusal of it may interest the reader:

After reading the long list of dignitaries, etc., and remembering the sparseness of the population, one is almost inclined to wonder where the material for that portion of the procession devoted to "Hawaiian Population Generally" is going to be procured:

Undertaker.

Royal School. Kawaiahao School. Roman Catholic School.

Miaemae School.

Honolulu Fire Department.
Mechanics' Benefit Union.
Attending Physicians.
Konohikis (Superintendents) of the Crown Lands, Konohikis of the
Private Lands of His Majesty* Konohikis of Private Lands of Her late
Royal Highness.
Governor of Oahu and Staff.
Hulumanu (Military Company)
Household Troops.
The Prince of Hawaii's Own (Military Company)
The King's household servants.
Servants of Her late Royal Highness.
Protestant Clergy. The Clergy of the Roman Catholic Church.
His Lordship Louis Maigret, The Right Rev. Bishop of Arathea,
Vicar-Apostolic of the Hawaiian Islands.
The Clergy of the Hawaiian Reformed Catholic Church.
His Lordship the Right Rev. Bishop of Honolulu.

Escort Hawaiian Cavalry.		Escort Hawaiian Cavalry.
Large Kahilis.	[HEARSE]	Large Kahilis.*
Small Kahilis.		Small Kahilis.
Pall Bearers.		Pall Bearers.

Her Majesty Queen Emma's Carriage.
His Majesty's Staff.
Carriage of Her late Royal Highness.
Carriage of Her Majesty the Queen Dowager.
The King's Chancellor.
Cabinet Ministers.
His Excellency the Minister Resident of the United States.
H. L. M's Commissioner.
H B. M's Acting Commissioner.
Judges of Supreme Court.
Privy Councillors.
Members of Legislative Assembly.
Consular Corps.
Circuit Judges.
Clerks of Government Departments.
Members of the Bar.
Collector General, Custom-house Officers and Officers of the Customs.
Marshal and Sheriffs of the different Islands.
King's Yeomanry.
Foreign Residents.
Ahahui Kaahumanu.
Hawaiian Population Generally.

*Ranks of long-handled mops made of gaudy feathers—sacred to royalty.
They are stuck in the ground around the tomb and left there.

Hawaiian Cavalry.
Police Force.

I resume my journal at the point where the procession arrived at the royal mausoleum:

As the procession filed through the gate, the military deployed handsomely to the right and left and formed an avenue through which the long column of mourners passed to the tomb. The coffin was borne through the door of the mausoleum, followed by the King and his chiefs, the great officers of the kingdom, foreign Consuls, Embassadors and distinguished guests (Burlingame and General Van Valkenburgh). Several of the kahilis were then fastened to a frame-work in front of the tomb, there to remain until they decay and fall to pieces, or, forestalling this, until another scion of royalty dies. At this point of the proceedings the multitude set up such a heart-broken wailing as I hope never to hear again. The soldiers fired three volleys of musketry—the wailing being previously silenced to permit of the guns being heard. His Highness Prince William, in a showy military uniform (the "true prince," this—scion of the house over-thrown by the present dynasty—he was formerly betrothed to the Princess but was not allowed to marry her), stood guard and paced back and forth within the door. The privileged few who followed the coffin into the mausoleum remained sometime, but the King soon came out and stood in the door and near one side of it. A stranger could have guessed his rank (although he was so simply and unpretentiously dressed) by the profound deference paid him by all persons in his vicinity; by seeing his high officers receive his quiet orders and suggestions with bowed and uncovered heads and by observing how careful those persons who came out of the mausoleum were to avoid "crowding" him (although there was room enough in the doorway for a wagon to pass, for that matter); how respectfully they edged out sideways, scraping their backs against the wall and always presenting a front view of their persons to his Majesty, and never putting their hats on until they were well out of the royal presence.

He was dressed entirely in black—dress-coat and silk hat—and looked rather democratic in the midst of the showy uniforms about him. On his breast he wore a large gold star, which was half hidden by the lappel of his coat. He remained at the door a half hour, and occasionally gave an order to the men who were erecting the kahilis before the tomb. He had the good taste to make one of them substitute black crepe for the ordinary hempen rope he was about to tie one of them to the frame-work with. Finally he entered his carriage and drove away, and the populace shortly began to drop into his wake. While he was in view there was but one man who attracted more attention than himself, and that was Harris (the Yankee Prime Minister). This feeble personage had crepe enough around his hat to express the grief of an entire nation, and as usual he neglected no opportunity of making himself conspicuous and exciting the admiration of the simple Kanakas. Oh! noble ambition of this modern Richelieu!

It is interesting to contrast the funeral ceremonies of the Princess Victoria with those of her noted ancestor Kamehameha the Conqueror, who died fifty years ago-in 1819, the year before the first missionaries came.

"On the 8th of May, 1819, at the age of sixty-six, he died, as he had lived, in the faith of his country. It was his misfortune not to have come in contact with men who could have rightly influenced his religious aspirations. Judged by his advantages and compared with the most eminent of his countrymen he may be justly styled not only great, but good. To this day his memory warms the heart and elevates the national feelings of Hawaiians. They are proud of their old warrior King; they love his name; his deeds form their historical age; and an enthusiasm everywhere prevails, shared even by foreigners who knew his worth, that constitutes the firmest pillar of the throne of his dynasty.

"In lieu of human victims (the custom of that age), a sacrifice of three hundred dogs attended his obsequies—no mean holocaust when their national value and the estimation in which they were held are considered. The bones of Kamehameha, after being kept for a while, were so carefully concealed that all knowledge of their final resting place is now lost. There was a proverb current among the common people that the bones of a cruel King could not be hid; they made fish-hooks and arrows of them, upon which, in using them, they vented their abhorrence of his memory in bitter execrations."

The account of the circumstances of his death, as written by the native historians, is full of minute detail, but there is scarcely a line of it which does not mention or illustrate some by-gone custom of the country. In this respect it is the most comprehensive document I have yet met with. I will quote it entire:

"When Kamehameha was dangerously sick, and the priests were unable to cure him, they said: `Be of good courage and build a house for the god' (his own private god or idol), that thou mayest recover.' The chiefs corroborated this advice of the priests, and a place of worship was prepared for Kukailimoku, and consecrated in the evening. They proposed also to the

King, with a view to prolong his life, that human victims should be sacrificed to his deity; upon which the greater part of the people absconded through fear of death, and concealed themselves in hiding places till the tabu* in which destruction impended, was past. It is doubtful whether Kamehameha approved of the plan of the chiefs and priests to sacrifice men, as he was known to say, `The men are sacred for the King;' meaning that they were for the service of his successor. This information was derived from Liholiho, his son.

"After this, his sickness increased to such a degree that he had not strength to turn himself in his bed. When another season, consecrated for worship at the new temple (heiau) arrived, he said to his son, Liholiho, `Go thou and make supplication to thy god; I am not able to go, and will offer my prayers at home.' When his devotions to his feathered god, Kukailimoku, were concluded, a certain religiously disposed individual who had a bird god, suggested to the King that through its influence his sickness might be removed. The name of this god was Pua; its body was made of a bird, now eaten by the Hawaiians, and called in their language alae. Kamehameha was willing that a trial should be made, and two houses were constructed to facilitate the experiment; but while dwelling in them he became so very weak as not to receive food. After lying there three days, his wives, children and chiefs, perceiving that he was very low, returned him to his own house. In the evening he was carried to the eating house,† where he took a little food in his mouth which he did not swallow; also a cup of water. The chiefs requested him to give them his counsel; but he made no reply, and was carried back to the dwelling house; but when near midnight—ten o'clock, perhaps—he was carried again to the place to eat; but, as before, he merely tasted of what was presented to him. Then Kaikioewa addressed him thus: `Here we all are, your younger brethren, your son Liholiho and your foreigner; impart to us your dying charge, that Liholiho and Kaahumanu may hear.' Then Kamehameha inquired, `What do you say?' Kaikioewa repeated, `Your counsels for us.'

He then added, 'Move on in my good way and—.' He could proceed no further. The foreigner, Mr. Young, embraced and kissed him. Hoapili also embraced him, whispering something in his ear, after which he was taken back to the house. About twelve he was carried once more to the house for eating, into which his head entered, while his body was in the dwelling house immediately adjoining. It should be remarked that this frequent carrying of a sick chief from one house to another resulted from the tabu system, then in force. There were at that time six houses (huts) connected

*Tabu (pronounced tah-boo,) means prohibition (we have borrowed it,) or sacred. The tabu was sometimes permanent, sometimes temporary; and the person or thing placed under tabu was for the time being sacred to the purpose for which it was set apart. In the above case the victims selected under the tabu would be sacred to the sacrifice.

†It was deemed pollution to eat in the same hut a person slept in—the fact that the patient was dying could not modify the rigid etiquette.

with an establishment—one was for worship, one for the men to eat in, an eating house for the women, a house to sleep in, a house in which to manufacture kapa (native cloth) and one where, at certain intervals, the women might dwell in seclusion.

"The sick was once more taken to his house, when he expired; this was at two o'clock, a circumstance from which Leleiohoku derived his name. As he breathed his last, Kalaimoku came to the eating house to order those in it to go out. There were two aged persons thus directed to depart; one went, the other remained on account of love to the King, by whom he had formerly been kindly sustained. The children also were sent away. Then Kalaimoku came to the house, and the chiefs had a consultation. One of them spoke thus: `This is my thought—we will eat him raw.'* Kaahumanu (one of the dead King's widows) replied, `Perhaps his body is not at our disposal; that is more properly with his successor. Our part in him—his breath—has departed; his remains will be disposed of by Liholiho.'

"After this conversation the body was taken into the consecrated house for the performance of the proper rites by the priest and the new King. The name of this ceremony is uko; and when the sacred hog was baked the priest offered it to the dead body, and it became a god, the King at the same time repeating the customary prayers.

"Then the priest, addressing himself to the King and chiefs, said: `I will now make known to you the rules to be observed respecting persons to be sacrificed on the burial of this body. If you obtain one man before the corpse is removed, one will be sufficient; but after it leaves this house four will be required. If delayed until we carry the corpse to the grave there must be ten; but after it is deposited in the grave there must be fifteen. To-morrow morning there will be a tabu, and, if the sacrifice be delayed until that time, forty men must die.'

"Then the high priest, Hewahewa, inquired of the chiefs, `Where shall be the residence of King Liholiho?' They replied, `Where, indeed? You, of all men, ought to know.' Then the priest observed, `There are two suitable places; one is Kau, the other is Kohala.' The chiefs preferred the latter, as it was more thickly inhabited. The priest added, `These are proper places for the King's residence; but he must not remain in Kona, for it is polluted.' This was agreed to. It was now break of day. As he was being carried to the place of burial the people perceived that their King was dead, and they wailed. When the corpse was removed from the house to the tomb, a distance of one chain, the procession was met by a certain man who was ardently attached to the deceased. He leaped upon the chiefs who were carrying the King's body; he desired to die with him on account of his love. The chiefs drove him away. He persisted in making numerous attempts,

*This sounds suspicious, in view of the fact that all Sandwich Island historians, white and black, protest that cannibalism never existed in the islands. However, since they only proposed to "eat him raw" we "wont count that". But it would certainly have been cannibalism if they had cooked him.—
[M.T.]

which were unavailing. Kalaimoku also had it in his heart to die with him, but was prevented by Hookio.

"The morning following Kamehameha's death, Liholiho and his train departed for Kohala, according to the suggestions of the Priest, to avoid the defilement occasioned by the dead. At this time if a chief died the land was polluted, and the heirs sought a residence in another part of the country until the corpse was dissected and the bones tied in a bundle, which being done, the season of defilement terminated. If the deceased were not a chief, the house only was defiled which became pure again on the burial of the body. Such were the laws on this subject.

"On the morning on which Liholiho sailed in his canoe for Kohala, the chiefs and people mourned after their manner on occasion of a chief's death, conducting themselves like madmen and like beasts. Their conduct was such as to forbid description; The priests, also, put into action the sorcery apparatus, that the person who had prayed the King to death might die; for it was not believed that Kamehameha's departure was the effect either of sickness or old age. When the sorcerers set up by their fire-places stick with a strip of kapa flying at the top, the chief Keeaumoku, Kaahumanu's brother, came in a state of intoxication and broke the flag-staff of the sorcerers, from which it was inferred that Kaahumanu and her friends had been instrumental in the King's death. On this account they were subjected to abuse."

You have the contrast, now, and a strange one it is. This great Queen, Kaahumanu, who was "subjected to abuse" during the frightful orgies that followed the King's death, in accordance with ancient custom, afterward became a devout Christian and a steadfast and powerful friend of the missionaries.

Dogs were, and still are, reared and fattened for food, by the natives—hence the reference to their value in one of the above paragraphs.

Forty years ago it was the custom in the Islands to suspend all law for a certain number of days after the death of a royal personage; and then a saturnalia ensued which one may picture to himself after a fashion, but not in the full horror of the reality. The people shaved their heads, knocked out a tooth or two, plucked out an eye sometimes, cut, bruised, mutilated or burned their flesh, got drunk, burned each other's huts, maimed or murdered one another according to the caprice of the moment, and both sexes gave themselves up to brutal and unbridled licentiousness. And after it all, came a torpor from which the nation slowly emerged bewildered and dazed, as if from a hideous half-remembered nightmare. They were not the salt of the earth, those "gentle children of the sun."

The natives still keep up an old custom of theirs which cannot be comforting to an invalid. When they think a sick friend is going to die, a couple of dozen neighbors surround his hut and keep up a deafening wailing night and day till he either dies or gets well. No doubt this arrangement has helped many a subject to a shroud before his appointed time.

They surround a hut and wail in the same heart-broken way when its occupant returns from a journey. This is their dismal idea of a welcome. A very little of it would go a great way with most of us.

Chapter VII

Bound for Hawaii (a hundred and fifty miles distant,) to visit the great volcano and behold the other notable things which distinguish that island above the remainder of the group, we sailed from Honolulu on a certain Saturday afternoon, in the good schooner Boomerang.

The Boomerang was about as long as two street cars, and about as wide as one. She was so small (though she was larger than the majority of the inter-island coasters) that when I stood on her deck I felt but little smaller than the Colossus of Rhodes must have felt when he had a man-of-war under him. I could reach the water when she lay over under a strong breeze. When the Captain and my comrade (a Mr. Billings), myself and four other persons were all assembled on the little after portion of the deck which is sacred to the cabin passengers, it was full—there was not room for any more quality folks. Another section of the deck, twice as large as ours, was full of natives of both sexes, with their customary dogs, mats, blankets, pipes, calabashes of poi, fleas, and other luxuries and baggage of minor importance. As soon as we set sail the natives all lay down on the deck as thick as negroes in a slave-pen, and smoked, conversed, and spit on each other, and were truly amiable.

The little low-ceiled cabin below was rather larger than a hearse, and as dark as a vault. It had two coffins on each side—I mean two bunks. A small table, capable of accommodating three persons at dinner, stood against the forward bulkhead, and over it hung the dingiest whale oil lantern that ever peopled the obscurity of a dungeon with ghostly shapes. The floor room unoccupied was not extensive. One might swing a cat in it, perhaps, but not a long cat. The hold forward of the bulkhead had but little freight in it, and from morning till night a portly old rooster, with a voice like Baalam's ass, and the same disposition to use it, strutted up and down in that part of the vessel and crowed. He usually took dinner at six o'clock, and then, after an hour devoted to meditation, he mounted a barrel and crowed a good part of the night. He got hoarser and hoarser all the time, but he scorned to allow any personal consideration to interfere with his duty, and kept up his labors in defiance of threatened diphtheria.

Sleeping was out of the question when he was on watch. He was a source of genuine aggravation and annoyance. It was worse than useless to shout at him or apply offensive epithets to him—he only took these things for applause, and strained himself to make more noise. Occasionally, during the day, I threw potatoes at him through an aperture in the bulkhead, but he only dodged and went on crowing.

The first night, as I lay in my coffin, idly watching the dim lamp swinging to the rolling of the ship, and snuffing the nauseous odors of bilge water, I felt something gallop over me. I turned out promptly. However, I turned in again when I found it was only a rat. Presently something galloped over me once more. I knew it was not a rat this time, and I thought it might be a centipede, because the Captain had killed one on deck in the afternoon. I turned out. The first glance at the pillow showed me a repulsive sentinel perched upon each end of it—cockroaches as large as peach leaves—fellows with long, quivering antennae and fiery, malignant eyes. They were grating their teeth like tobacco worms, and appeared to be dissatisfied about something. I had often heard that these reptiles were in the habit of eating off sleeping sailors' toe nails down to the quick, and I would not get in the bunk any more. I lay down on the floor. But a rat came and bothered me, and shortly afterward a procession of cockroaches arrived and camped in my hair. In a few moments the rooster was crowing with uncommon spirit and a party of fleas were throwing double somersaults about my person in the wildest disorder, and taking a bite every time they struck. I was beginning to feel really annoyed. I got up and put my clothes on and went on deck.

The above is not overdrawn; it is a truthful sketch of inter-island schooner life. There is no such thing as keeping a vessel in elegant condition, when she carries molasses and Kanakas.

It was compensation for my sufferings to come unexpectedly upon so beautiful a scene as met my eye—to step suddenly out of the sepulchral gloom of the cabin and stand under the strong light of the moon—in the centre, as it were, of a glittering sea of liquid silver—to see the broad sails straining in the gale, the ship keeled over on her side, the angry foam hissing past her lee bulwarks, and sparkling sheets of spray dashing high over her bows and raining upon her decks; to brace myself and hang fast to the first object that presented itself, with hat jammed down and coat tails whipping in the breeze, and feel that exhilaration that thrills in one's hair and quivers down his back bone when he knows that every inch of canvas is drawing and the vessel cleaving through the waves at her utmost speed. There was no darkness, no dimness, no obscurity there. All was brightness, every object was vividly defined. Every prostrate Kanaka; every coil of rope; every calabash of poi; every puppy; every seam in the flooring; every bolthead; every object, however minute, showed sharp and distinct in its every outline; and the shadow of the broad mainsail lay black as a pall upon the deck, leaving Billings's white upturned face glorified and his body in a total eclipse.

Monday morning we were close to the island of Hawaii. Two of its high mountains were in view—Mauna Loa and Hualaiai. The latter is an imposing peak, but being only ten thousand feet high is seldom mentioned or heard of. Mauna Loa is said to be sixteen thousand feet high. The rays of glittering snow and ice, that clasped its summit like a claw, looked refreshing when viewed from the blistering climate we were in. One could stand on that mountain (wrapped up in blankets and furs to keep warm), and while he nibbled a snowball or an icicle to quench his thirst he could look down the long sweep of its sides and see spots where plants are growing that grow only where the bitter cold of Winter prevails; lower down he could see sections devoted to productions that thrive in the temperate zone alone; and at the bottom of the mountain he could see the home of the tufted cocoa-palms and other species of vegetation that grow only in the sultry atmosphere of eternal Summer. He could see all the climes of the world at a single glance of the eye, and that glance would only pass over a distance of four or five miles as the bird flies!

By and by we took boat and went ashore at Kailua, designing to ride horseback through the pleasant orange and coffee region of Kona, and rejoin the vessel at a point some leagues distant. This journey is well worth taking. The tram passes along on high ground—say a thousand feet above sea level and usually about a mile distant from the ocean, which is always in sight, save that occasionally you find yourself buried in the forest in the midst of a rank tropical vegetation and a dense growth of trees, whose great bows overarch the road and shut out sun and sea and everything, and leave you in a dim, shady tunnel, haunted with invisible singing birds and fragrant with the odor of flowers. It was pleasant to ride occasionally in the warm sun, and feast the eye upon the ever-changing panorama of the forest (beyond and below us), with its many tints, its softened lights and shadows, its billowy undulations sweeping gently down from the mountain to the sea. It was pleasant also, at intervals, to leave the sultry sun and pass into the cool, green depths of this forest and indulge in sentimental reflections under the inspiration of its brooding twilight and its whispering foliage.

We rode through one orange grove that had ten thousand trees in it! They were all laden with fruit.

At one farmhouse we got some large peaches of excellent flavor. This fruit, as a general thing, does not do well in the Sandwich Islands. It takes a sort of almond shape, and is small and bitter. It needs frost, they say, and perhaps it does; if this be so, it will have a good opportunity to go on needing it, as it will not be likely to get it. The trees from which the fine fruit I have spoken of, came, had been planted and replanted sixteen times, and to this treatment the proprietor of the orchard attributed his success.

We passed several sugar plantations—new ones and not very extensive. The crops were, in most cases, third rattoons. [Note.—The first crop is called "plant cane;" subsequent crops which spring from the original roots, without replanting, are called "rattoons."] Almost everywhere on the island of Hawaii sugar-cane matures in twelve months, both rattoons and plant, and although it ought to be taken off as soon as it tassels, no doubt, it is not absolutely necessary to do it until about four months afterward. In Kona, the average yield of an acre of ground is two tons of sugar, they say. This is only a moderate yield for these islands, but would be astounding for Louisiana and most other sugar growing countries. The plantations in Kona being on pretty high ground—up among the light and frequent rains—no irrigation whatever is required.

Chapter VIII

At four o'clock in the afternoon we were winding down a mountain of dreary and desolate lava to the sea, and closing our pleasant land journey. This lava is the accumulation of ages; one torrent of fire after another has rolled down here in old times, and built up the island structure higher and higher. Underneath, it is honey-combed with eaves; it would be of no use to dig wells in such a place; they would not hold water—you would not find any for them to hold, for that matter. Consequently, the planters depend upon cisterns.

The last lava flow occurred here so long ago that there are none now living who witnessed it. In one place it enclosed and burned down a grove of cocoa-nut trees, and the holes in the lava where the trunks stood are still visible; their sides retain the impression of the bark; the trees fell upon the burning river, and becoming partly submerged, left in it the perfect counterpart of every knot and branch and leaf, and even nut, for curiosity seekers of a long distant day to gaze upon and wonder at.

There were doubtless plenty of Kanaka sentinels on guard hereabouts at that time, but they did not leave casts of their figures in the lava as the Roman sentinels at Herculaneum and Pompeii did. It is a pity it is so, because such things are so interesting; but so it is. They probably went away. They went away early, perhaps. However, they had their merits; the Romans exhibited the higher pluck, but the Kanakas showed the sounder judgment.

Shortly we came in sight of that spot whose history is so familiar to every school-boy in the wide world—Kealakekua Bay—the place where Captain Cook, the great circumnavigator, was killed by the natives, nearly a hundred years ago. The setting sun was flaming upon it, a Summer shower was falling, and it was spanned by two magnificent rainbows. Two men who were in advance of us rode through one of these and for a moment their garments shone with a more than regal splendor. Why did not Captain Cook have taste enough to call his great discovery the Rainbow Islands? These charming spectacles are present to you at every turn; they are common in all the islands; they are visible every day, and frequently at night also—not the silvery bow we see once in an age in the States, by moonlight, but barred with all bright and beautiful colors, like the children of the sun and rain. I saw one of them a few nights ago. What the sailors call "raindogs"—little patches of rainbow—are often seen drifting about the heavens in these latitudes, like stained cathedral windows.

Kealakekua Bay is a little curve like the last kink of a snail-shell, winding deep into the land, seemingly not more than a mile wide from shore to shore. It is bounded on one side—where the murder was done—by a little flat plain, on which stands a cocoanut grove and some ruined houses; a steep wall of lava, a thousand feet high at the upper end and three or four hundred at the lower, comes down from the mountain and bounds the inner extremity of it. From this wall the place takes its name, Kealakekua, which in the native tongue signifies "The Pathway of the Gods." They say, (and still believe, in spite of their liberal education in Christianity), that the great god Lono, who used to live upon the hillside, always traveled that causeway when urgent business connected with heavenly affairs called him down to the seashore in a hurry.

As the red sun looked across the placid ocean through the tall, clean stems of the cocoanut trees, like a blooming whiskey bloat through the bars of a city prison, I went and stood in the edge of the water on the flat rock pressed by Captain Cook's feet when the blow was dealt which took away his life, and tried to picture in my mind the doomed man struggling in the midst of the multitude of exasperated savages—the men in the ship crowding to the vessel's side and gazing in anxious dismay toward the shore—the—but I discovered that I could not do it.

It was growing dark, the rain began to fall, we could see that the distant Boomerang was helplessly becalmed at sea, and so I adjourned to the cheerless little box of a warehouse and sat down to smoke and think, and wish the ship would make the land—for we had not eaten much for ten hours and were viciously hungry.

Plain unvarnished history takes the romance out of Captain Cook's assassination, and renders a deliberate verdict of justifiable homicide. Wherever he went among the islands, he was cordially received and welcomed by the inhabitants, and his ships lavishly supplied with all manner of food. He returned these kindnesses with insult and ill-treatment. Perceiving that the people took him for the long vanished and lamented god Lono, he encouraged them in the delusion for the sake of the limitless power it gave him; but during the famous disturbance at this spot, and while he and his comrades were surrounded by fifteen thousand maddened savages, he received a hurt and betrayed his earthly origin with a groan.

It was his death-warrant. Instantly a shout went up: "He groans!—he is not a god!" So they closed in upon him and dispatched him.

His flesh was stripped from the bones and burned (except nine pounds of it which were sent on board the ships). The heart was hung up in a native hut, where it was found and eaten by three children, who mistook it for the heart of a dog. One of these children grew to be a very old man, and died in Honolulu a few years ago. Some of Cook's bones were recovered and consigned to the deep by the officers of the ships.

Small blame should attach to the natives for the killing of Cook. They treated him well. In return, he abused them. He and his men inflicted bodily injury upon many of them at different times, and killed at least three of them before they offered any proportionate retaliation.

Near the shore we found "Cook's Monument"—only a cocoanut stump, four feet high and about a foot in diameter at the butt. It had lava boulders piled around its base to hold it up and keep it in its place, and it was entirely sheathed over, from top to bottom, with rough, discolored sheets of copper, such as ships' bottoms are coppered with. Each sheet had a rude inscription scratched upon it—with a nail, apparently—and in every case the execution was wretched. Most of these merely recorded the visits of British naval commanders to the spot, but one of them bore this legend:

"Near this spot fen
CAPTAIN JAMES COOK,
The Distinguished Circumnavigator, who Discovered these Islands A. D. 1778.

After Cook's murder, his second in command, on board the ship, opened fire upon the swarms of natives on the beach, and one of his cannon balls cut this cocoanut tree short off and left this monumental stump standing. It looked sad and lonely enough to us, out there in the rainy twilight. But there is no other monument to Captain Cook. True, up on the mountain side we had passed by a large inclosure like an ample hog-pen, built of lava blocks, which marks the spot where Cook's flesh was stripped from his bones and burned; but this is not properly a monument, since it was erected by the natives themselves, and less to do honor to the circumnavigator than for the sake of convenience in roasting him. A thing like a guide-board was elevated above this pen on a tall pole, and formerly there was an inscription upon it describing the memorable occurrence that had there taken place; but the sun and the wind have long ago so defaced it as to render it illegible.

Toward midnight a fine breeze sprang up and the schooner soon worked herself into the bay and cast anchor. The boat came ashore for us, and in a little while the clouds and the rain were all gone. The moon was beaming tranquilly down on land and sea, and we two were stretched upon the deck sleeping the refreshing sleep and dreaming the happy dreams that we only vouchsafed to the weary and the innocent.

Chapter IX

In the breezy morning we went ashore and visited the ruined temple of the last god Lono. The high chief cook of this temple—the priest who presided over it and roasted the human sacrifices—was uncle to Obookia, and at one time that youth was an apprentice-priest under him. Obookia was a young native of fine mind, who, together with three other native boys, was taken to New England by the captain of a whaleship during the reign of Kamehameha I, and they were the means of attracting the attention of the religious world to their country. This resulted in the sending of missionaries there. And this Obookia was the very same sensitive savage who sat down on the church steps and wept because his people did not have the Bible. That incident has been very elaborately painted in many a charming Sunday School book—aye, and told so plaintively and so tenderly that I have cried over it in Sunday School myself, on general principles, although at a time when I did not know much and could not understand why the people of the Sandwich Islands needed to worry so much about it as long as they did not know there was a Bible at all.

Obookia was converted and educated, and was to have

returned to his native land with the first missionaries, had he lived. The other native youths made the voyage, and two of them did good service, but the third, William Kanui, fen from grace afterward, for a time, and when the gold excitement broke out in California he journeyed thither and went to mining, although he was fifty years old. He succeeded pretty well, but the failure of Page, Bacon & Co. relieved him of six thousand dollars, and then, to all intents and purposes, he was a bankrupt in his old age and he resumed service in the pulpit again. He died in Honolulu in 1864.

Quite a broad tract of land near the temple, extending from the sea to the mountain top, was sacred to the god Lono in olden times—so sacred that if a common native set his sacrilegious foot upon it it was judicious for him to make his will, because his time had come. He might go around it by water, but he could not cross it. It was well sprinkled with pagan temples and stocked with awkward, homely idols carved out of logs of wood. There was a temple devoted to prayers for rain—and with fine sagacity it was placed at a point so well up on the mountain side that if you prayed there twenty-four times a day for rain you would be likely to get it every time. You would seldom get to your Amen before you would have to hoist your umbrella.

And there was a large temple near at band which was built in a single night, in the midst of storm and thunder and rain, by the ghastly hands of dead men! Tradition says that by the weird glare of the lightning a noiseless multitude of phantoms were seen at their strange labor far up the mountain side at dead of night—flitting hither and thither and bearing great lava-blocks clasped in their nerveless fingers—appearing and disappearing as the pallid lustre fell upon their forms and faded away again. Even to this day, it is said, the natives hold this dread structure in awe and reverence, and will not pass by it in the night.

At noon I observed a bevy of nude native young ladies bathing in the sea, and went and sat down on their clothes to keep them from being stolen. I begged them to come out, for the sea was rising and I was satisfied that they were running some risk. But they were not afraid, and presently went on with their sport. They were finished swimmers and divers, and enjoyed themselves to the last degree. They swam races, splashed and ducked and tumbled each other about, and filled the air with their laughter. It is said that the first thing an Islander learns is how to swim; learning to walk being a matter of smaller consequence, comes afterward. One hears tales of native men and women swimming ashore from vessels many miles at sea—more miles, indeed, than I dare vouch for or even mention. And they tell of a native diver who went down in thirty or forty-foot waters and brought up an anvil! I think he swallowed the anvil afterward, if my memory serves me. However I will not urge this point.

I have spoken, several times, of the god Lono—I may well furnish two or three sentences concerning him.

The idol the natives worshiped for him was a slender, unornamented staff twelve feet long. Tradition says he was a favorite god on the Island of Hawaii—a great king who had been deified for meritorious services—just our own fashion of rewarding heroes, with the difference that we would have made him a Postmaster instead of a god, no doubt. In an angry moment he slew his wife, a goddess named Kaikilani Aiii. Remorse of conscience drove him mad, and tradition presents us the singular spectacle of a god traveling "on the shoulder;" for in his gnawing grief be wandered about from place to place boxing and wrestling with all whom he met. Of course this pastime soon lost its novelty, inasmuch as it must necessarily have been the case that when so powerful a deity sent a frail human opponent "to grass" he never came back any more. Therefore, he instituted games called makahiki, and ordered that they should be held in his honor, and then sailed for foreign lands on a three cornered raft, stating that he would return some day—and that was the last of Lono. He was never seen any more; his raft got swamped, perhaps. But the people always expected his return, and thus they were easily led to accept Captain Cook as the restored god.

Some of the old natives believed Cook was Lono to the day of their death; but many did not, for they could not understand how he could die if he was a god.

Only mile or so from Kealakekua Bay is a spot of historic interest—the place where the last battle was fought for idolatry. Of course we visited it, and came away as wise as most people do who go and gaze upon such mementoes of the past when in an unreflective mood.

While the first missionaries were on their way around the Horn, the idolatrous customs which had obtained in the island, as far back as tradition reached were suddenly broken up. Old Kamehameha I., was dead, and his son, Liholiho, the new King was a free liver, a roystering, dissolute fellow, and hated the restraints of the ancient tabu. His assistant in the Government, Kaahumanu, the Queen dowager, was proud and high-spirited, and hated the tabu because it restricted the privileges of her sex and degraded all women very nearly to the level of brutes. So the case stood. Liholiho had half a mind to put his foot down, Kaahumanu had a whole mind to badger him into doing it, and whiskey did the rest. It was probably the rest. It was probably the first time whiskey ever prominently figured as an aid to civilization. Lilioliho came up to Kailua as drunk as a piper, and attended a great feast; the determined Queen spurred his drunken courage up to a reckless pitch, and then, while all the multitude stared in blank dismay, he moved deliberately forward and sat down with the women! They saw him eat from the same vessel with them, and were appalled! Terrible moments drifted slowly by, and still the King ate, still he lived, still the lightnings of the insulted gods were withheld! Then conviction came like a revelation—the superstitions of a hundred generations passed from before the people like a cloud, and a shout went up, "the tabu is broken! the tabu is broken!"

Thus did King Liholiho and his dreadful whiskey preach the first sermon and prepare the way for the new gospel that was speeding southward over the waves of the Atlantic.

The tabu broken and destruction failing to follow the awful sacrilege, the people, with that childlike precipitancy which has always characterized them, jumped to the conclusion that their gods were a weak and wretched swindle, just as they formerly jumped to the conclusion that Captain Cook was no god, merely because he groaned, and promptly killed him without stopping to inquire whether a god might not groan as well as a man if it suited his convenience to do it; and satisfied that the idols were powerless to protect themselves they went to work at once and pulled them down—hacked them to pieces—applied the torch—annihilated them!

The pagan priests were furious. And well they might be; they had held the fattest offices in the land, and now they were beggared; they had been great—they had stood above the chiefs—and now they were vagabonds. They raised a revolt; they seared a number of people into joining their standard, and Bekuokalani, an ambitious offshoot of royalty, was easily persuaded to become their leader.

In the first skirmish the idolaters triumphed over the royal army sent against them, and full of confidence they resolved to march upon Kailua. The King sent an envoy to try and conciliate them, and came very near being an envoy short by the operation; the savages not only refused to listen to him, but wanted to kill him. So the King sent his men forth under Major General Kalaimoku and the two hosts met at Kuamoo. The battle was long and fierce—men and women fighting side by aide, as was the custom—and when the day was done the rebels were flying in every direction in hopeless panic, and idolatry and the tabu were dead in the land!

The royalists marched gayly home to Kailua glorifying the new dispensation. "There is no power in the gods," said they; they are a vanity and a lie. The army with idols was weak; the army without idols was strong and victorious!"

The nation was without a religion.

The missionary ship arrived in safety shortly afterward, timed by providential exactness to meet the emergency, and the Gospel was planted as in a virgin soil.

Chapter X

At noon, we hired a Kanaka to take us down to the ancient ruins at Honaunau in his canoe—price two dollars—reasonable enough, for a sea voyage of eight miles, counting both ways.

The native canoe is an irresponsible looking contrivance. I cannot think of anything to liken it to but a boy's sled runner hollowed out, and that does not quite convey the correct idea. It is about fifteen feet long, high and pointed at both ends, is a foot and a half or two feet deep, and so narrow that if you wedged a fat man into it you might not get him out again. It sits on top of the water like a duck, but it has an outrigger and does not upset easily, if you keep still. This outrigger is formed of two long bent sticks like plow handles, which project from one side, and to their outer ends is bound a curved beam composed of an extremely light wood, which skims along the surface of the water and thus saves you from an upset on that side, while the outrigger's weight is not so easily lifted as to make an upset on the other side a thing to be greatly feared. Still, until one gets used to sitting perched upon this knife-blade, he is apt to reason within himself that it would be more comfortable if there were just an outrigger or so on the other side also.

I had the bow seat, and Billings sat amidships and faced the Kanaka, who occupied the stem of the craft and did the paddling. With the first stroke the trim shell of a thing shot out from the shore like an arrow. There was not much to see. While we were on the shallow water of the reef, it was pastime to look down into the limpid depths at the large bunches of branching coral—the unique shrubbery of the sea. We lost that, though, when we got out into the dead blue water of the deep. But we had the picture of the surf, then, dashing angrily against the crag-bound shore and sending a foaming spray high into the air. There was interest in this beetling border, too, for it was honey-combed with quaint eaves and arches and tunnels, and had a rude semblance of the dilapidated architecture of ruined keeps and castles rising out of the restless sea. When this novelty ceased to be a novelty, we turned our eyes shoreward and gazed at the long mountain with its rich green forests stretching up into the curtaining clouds, and at the specks of houses in the rearward distance and the diminished schooner riding sleepily at anchor. And when these grew tiresome we dashed boldly into the midst of a school of huge, beastly porpoises engaged at their eternal game of arching over a wave and disappearing, and then doing it over again and keeping it up—always circling over, in that way, like so many well- submerged wheels. But the porpoises wheeled themselves away, and then we were thrown upon our own resources. It did not take many minutes to discover that the sun was blazing like a bonfire, and that the weather was of a melting temperature. It had a drowsing effect, too.

In one place we came upon a large company of naked natives, of both sexes and all ages, amusing themselves with the national pastime of surf-bathing. Each heathen would paddle three or four hundred yards out to sea, (taking a short board with him), then face the shore and wait for a particularly prodigious billow to come along; at the right moment he would fling his board upon its foamy crest and himself upon the board, and here he would come whizzing by like a bombshell! It did not seem that a lightning express train could shoot along at a more hair-lifting speed. I tried surf-bathing once, subsequently, but made a failure of it. I got the board placed right, and at the right moment, too; but missed the connection myself.—The board struck the shore in three quarters of a second, without any cargo, and I struck the bottom about the same time, with a couple of barrels of water in me. None but natives ever master the art of surf-bathing thoroughly.

At the end of an hour, we had made the four miles, and landed on a level point of land, upon which was a wide extent of old ruins, with many a tall cocoanut tree growing among them. Here was the ancient City of Refuge—a vast inclosure, whose stone walls were twenty feet thick at the base, and fifteen feet high; an oblong square, a thousand and forty feet one way and a fraction under seven hundred the other. Within this inclosure, in early times, has been three rude temples; each two hundred and ten feet long by one hundred wide, and thirteen high.

In those days, if a man killed another anywhere on the island the relatives were privileged to take the murderers life; and then a chase for life and liberty began—the outlawed criminal flying through pathless forests and over mountain and plain, with his hopes fixed upon the protecting walls of the City of Refuge, and the avenger of blood following hotly after him! Sometimes the race was kept up to the very gates of the temple, and the panting pair sped through long files of excited natives, who watched the contest with flashing eye and dilated nostril, encouraging the hunted refugee with sharp, inspiriting ejaculations, and sending up a ringing

shout of exultation when the saving gates closed upon him
and the cheated pursuer sank exhausted at the threshold.
But sometimes the flying criminal fell under the hand of the
avenger at the very door, when one more brave stride, one
more brief second of time would have brought his feet upon
the sacred ground and barred him against all harm. Where
did these isolated pagans get this idea of a City of Refuge—
this ancient Oriental custom? This old sanctuary was sacred
to all—even to rebels in arms and invading armies. Once
within its walls, and confession made to the priest and
absolution obtained, the wretch with a price upon his head
could go forth without fear and without danger—he was
tabu, and to harm him was death. The routed rebels in the
lost battle for idolatry fled to this place to claim sanctuary,
and many were thus saved.

Close to the corner of the great inclosure is a round
structure of stone, some six or eight feet high, with a level
top about ten or twelve in diameter. This was the place of
execution. A high palisade of cocoanut piles shut out the
cruel scenes from the vulgar multitude. Here criminals were
killed, the flesh stripped from the bones and burned, and the
bones secreted in holes in the body of the structure. If the
man had been guilty of a high crime, the entire corpse was
burned.

The walls of the temple are a study. The same food for
speculation that is offered the visitor to the Pyramids of
Egypt he will find here—the mystery of how they were
constructed by a people unacquainted with science and
mechanics. The natives have no invention of their own for
hoisting heavy weights, they had no beasts of burden, and
they have never even shown any knowledge of the properties
of the lever. Yet some of the lava blocks quarried out,
brought over rough, broken ground, and built into this wall,
six or seven feet from the ground, are of prodigious size and

would weigh tons. How did they transport and how raise them?

Both the inner and outer surfaces of the walls present a smooth front and are very creditable specimens of masonry. The blocks are of all manner of shapes and sizes, but yet are fitted together with the neatest exactness. The gradual narrowing of the wall from the base upward is accurately preserved.

No cement was used, but the edifice is firm and compact and is capable of resisting storm and decay for centuries. Who built this temple, and how was it built, and when, are mysteries that may never be unraveled.

Outside of these ancient walls lies a sort of coffin-shaped stone eleven feet four inches long and three feet square at the small end (it would weigh a few thousand pounds), which the high chief who held sway over this district many centuries ago brought thither on his shoulder one day to use as a lounge! This circumstance is established by the most reliable traditions. He used to lie down on it, in his indolent way, and keep all eye on his subjects at work for him and see that there was no "soldiering" done. And no doubt there was not any done to speak of, because he was a man of that sort of build that incites to attention to business on the part of an employee. He was fourteen or fifteen feet high. When he stretched himself at full length on his lounge, his legs hung down over the end, and when he snored he woke the dead. These facts are all attested by irrefragable tradition.

On the other side of the temple is a monstrous seven-ton rock, eleven feet long, seven feet wide and three feet thick. It is raised a foot or a foot and a half above the ground, and rests upon half a dozen little stony pedestals. The same old fourteen-footer brought it down from the mountain, merely for fun (he had his own notions about fun), and propped it up as we find it now and as others may find it a century hence, for it would take a score of horses to budge it from its position. They say that fifty or sixty years ago the proud Queen Kaahumanu used to fly to this rock for safety, whenever she had been making trouble with her fierce husband, and hide under it until his wrath was appeased. But these Kanakas will lie, and this statement is one of their ablest efforts—for Kaahumanu was six feet high—she was bulky—she was built like an ox-and she could no more have squeezed herself under that rock than she could have passed between the cylinders of a sugar mill. What could she gain by it, even if she succeeded? To be chased and abased by a savage husband could not be otherwise than humiliating to her high spirit, yet it could never make her feel so flat as an hour's repose under that rock would.

We walked a mile over a raised macadamized road of uniform width; a road paved with flat stones and exhibiting in its every detail a considerable degree of engineering skill. Some say that that wise old pagan, Kamehameha I. planned and built it, but others say it was built so long before his time that the knowledge of who constructed it has passed out of the traditions. In either case, however, as the handiwork of an untaught and degraded race it is a thing of pleasing interest. The stones are worn and smooth, and pushed apart in places, so that the road has the exact appearance of those ancient paved highways leading out of Rome which one sees in pictures.

The object of our tramp was to visit a great natural curiosity at the base of the foothills—a congealed cascade of lava. Some old forgotten volcanic eruption sent its broad river of fire down the mountain side here, and it poured down in a great torrent from an overhanging bluff some fifty feet high to the ground below. The flaming torrent cooled in the winds from the sea, and remains there to-day, all seamed, and frothed and rippled a petrified Niagara. It is very picturesque, and withal so natural that one might almost imagine it still flowed. A smaller stream trickled over the cliff and built up an isolated pyramid about thirty feet high, which has the semblance of a mass of large gnarled and knotted vines and roots and stems intricately twisted and woven together.

We passed in behind the cascade and the pyramid, and found the bluff pierced by several cavernous tunnels, whose crooked courses we followed a long distance.

Two of these winding tunnels stand as proof of Nature's mining abilities. Their floors are level, they are seven feet wide, and their roofs are gently arched. Their height is not uniform, however. We passed through one a hundred feet long, which leads through a spur of the hill and opens out well up in the sheer wall of a precipice whose foot rests in the waves of the sea. It is a commodious tunnel, except that there are occasional places in it where one must stoop to pass under. The roof is lava, of course, and is thickly studded with little lava-pointed icicles an inch long, which hardened as they dripped. They project as closely together as the iron teeth of a corn-sheller, mid if one will stand up straight and walk any distance there, he can get his hair combed free of charge.

Chapter XI

We got back to the schooner in good time, and then sailed down to Kau, where we disembarked and took final leave of the vessel. Next day we bought horses and bent our way over the summer-clad mountain-terraces, toward the great volcano of Kilauea (Ke-low-way-ah). We made nearly a two days' journey of it, but that was on account of laziness. Toward sunset on the second day, we reached an elevation of some four thousand feet above sea level, and as we picked our careful way through billowy wastes of lava long generations ago stricken dead and cold in the climax of its tossing fury, we began to come upon signs of the near presence of the volcano—signs in the nature of ragged fissures that discharged jets of sulphurous vapor into the air, hot from the molten ocean down in the bowels of the mountain.

Shortly the crater came into view. I have seen Vesuvius since, but it was a mere toy, a child's volcano, a soup-kettle, compared to this. Mount Vesuvius is a shapely cone thirty-six hundred feet high; its crater an inverted cone only three hundred feet deep, and not more than a thousand feet in diameter, if as much as that; its rims meagre, modest, and docile.—But here was a vast, perpendicular, walled cellar, nine hundred feet deep in some places, thirteen hundred in others, level-floored, and ten miles in circumference! Here was a yawning pit upon whose floor the armies of Russia could camp, and have room to spare.

Perched upon the edge of the crater, at the opposite end from where we stood, was a small look-out house—say three miles away. It assisted us, by comparison, to comprehend and appreciate the great depth of the basin—it looked like a tiny martin-box clinging at the eaves of a cathedral. After some little time spent in resting and looking and ciphering, we hurried on to the hotel.

By the path it is half a mile from the Volcano House to the lookout-house. After a hearty supper we waited until it was thoroughly dark and then started to the crater. The first glance in that direction revealed a scene of wild beauty. There was a heavy fog over the crater and it was splendidly illuminated by the glare from the fires below. The illumination was two miles wide and a mile high, perhaps; and if you ever, on a dark night and at a distance beheld the light from thirty or

forty blocks of distant buildings all on fire at once, reflected strongly against overhanging clouds, you can form a fair idea of what this looked like.

A colossal column of cloud towered to a great height in the air immediately above the crater, and the outer swell of every one of its vast folds was dyed with a rich crimson luster, which was subdued to a pale rose tint in the depressions between. It glowed like a muffled torch and stretched upward to a dizzy height toward the zenith. I thought it just possible that its like had not been seen since the children of Israel wandered on their long march through the desert so many centuries ago over a path illuminated by the mysterious "pillar of fire." And I was sure that I now had a vivid conception of what the majestic "pillar of fire" was like, which almost amounted to a revelation.

Arrived at the little thatched lookout house, we rested our elbows on the railing in front and looked abroad over the wide crater and down over the sheer precipice at the seething fires beneath us. The view was a startling improvement on my daylight experience. I turned to see the effect on the balance of the company and found the reddest-faced set of men I almost ever saw. In the strong light every countenance glowed like red-hot iron, every shoulder was suffused with crimson and shaded rearward into dingy, shapeless obscurity! The place below looked like the infernal regions and these men like half-cooled devils just come up on a furlough.

I turned my eyes upon the volcano again. The "cellar" was tolerably well lighted up. For a mile and a half in front of us and half a mile on either side, the floor of the abyss was magnificently illuminated; beyond these limits the mists hung down their gauzy curtains and cast a deceptive gloom over all that made the twinkling fires in the remote corners of the crater seem countless leagues removed—made them seem like the camp-fires of a great army far away. Here was room for the imagination to work! You could imagine those lights the width of a continent away—and that hidden under the intervening darkness were hills, and winding rivers, and weary wastes of plain and desert—and even then the tremendous vista stretched on, and on, and on!—to the fires and far beyond! You could not compass it—it was the idea of eternity made tangible—and the longest end of it made visible to the naked eye!

The greater part of the vast floor of the desert under us was as black as ink, and apparently smooth and level; but over a mile square of it was ringed and streaked and striped with a thousand branching streams of liquid and gorgeously brilliant fire! It looked like a colossal railroad map of the State of Massachusetts done in chain lightning on a midnight sky. Imagine it—imagine a coal-black sky slivered into a tangled net-work of angry fire!

Here and there were gleaming holes a hundred feet in diameter, broken in the dark crust, and in them the melted lava—the color a dazzling white just tinged with yellow—was boiling and surging furiously; and from these holes branched numberless bright torrents in many directions, like the spokes of a wheel, and kept a tolerably straight course for a while and then swept round in huge rainbow curves, or made a long succession of sharp worm-fence angles, which looked precisely like the fiercest jagged lightning. These streams met other streams, and they mingled with and crossed and recrossed each other in every conceivable direction, like skate tracks on a popular skating ground. Sometimes streams twenty or thirty feet wide flowed from the holes to some distance without dividing—and through the opera-glasses we could see that they ran down small, steep hills and were genuine cataracts of fire, white at their source, but soon cooling and turning to the richest red, grained with alternate lines of black and gold. Every now and then masses of the dark crust broke away and floated slowly down these streams like rafts down a river. Occasionally the molten lava flowing under the superincumbent crust broke through—split a dazzling streak, from five hundred to a thousand feet long, like a sudden flash of lightning, and then acre after acre of the cold lava parted into fragments, turned up edgewise like cakes of ice when a great river breaks up, plunged downward and were swallowed in the crimson cauldron. Then the wide expanse of the "thaw" maintained a ruddy glow for a while, but shortly cooled and became black and level again. During a "thaw," every dismembered cake was marked by a glittering white border which was superbly shaded inward by aurora borealis rays, which were a flaming yellow where they joined the white border, and from thence toward their points tapered into glowing crimson, then into a rich, pale carmine, and finally into a faint blush that held its own a moment and then dimmed and turned black. Some of the streams preferred to mingle together in a tangle of fantastic circles, and then they looked something like the confusion of ropes one sees on a ship's deck when she has just taken in sail and dropped anchor—provided one can imagine those ropes on fire.

Through the glasses, the little fountains scattered about looked very beautiful. They boiled, and coughed, and splattered, and discharged sprays of stringy red fire—of about the consistency of mush, for instance—from ten to fifteen feet into the air, along with a shower of brilliant white sparks—a quaint and unnatural mingling of gouts of blood and snow-flakes! We had circles and serpents and streaks of lightning all twined and wreathed and tied together, without a break throughout an area more than a mile square (that amount of ground was covered, though it was not strictly "square"), and it was with a feeling of placid exultation that we reflected that many years had elapsed since any visitor had seen such a splendid display—since any visitor had seen anything more than the now snubbed and insignificant "North" and "South" lakes in action. We had been reading old files of Hawaiian newspapers and the "Record Book" at the Volcano House, and were posted.

I could see the North Lake lying out on the black floor away off in the outer edge of our panorama, and knitted to it by a web-work of lava streams. In its individual capacity it looked very little more respectable than a schoolhouse on fire. True, it was about nine hundred feet long and two or three hundred wide, but then, under the present circumstances, it necessarily appeared rather insignificant, and besides it was so distant from us.

I forgot to say that the noise made by the babbling lava is not great, heard as we heard it from our lofty perch. It makes three distinct sounds—a rushing, a hissing, and a coughing or puffing sound; and if you stand on the brink and close your eyes it is no trick at all to imagine that you are sweeping down a river on a large low-pressure steamer, and that you hear the hissing of the steam about her boilers, the puffing from her escape-pipes and the churning rush of the water abaft her wheels. The smell of sulphur is strong, but not unpleasant to a sinner.

We left the lookout house at ten o'clock in a half cooked condition, because of the heat from Pele's furnaces, and wrapping up in blankets, for the night was cold, we returned to our Hotel.

Chapter XII

The next night was appointed for a visit to the bottom of the crater, for we desired to traverse its floor and see the "North Lake" (of fire) which lay two miles away, toward the further wall. After dark half a dozen of us set out, with lanterns, and native guides, and climbed down a crazy, thousand-foot pathway in a crevice fractured in the crater wall, and reached the bottom in safety.

The irruption of the previous evening had spent its force and the floor looked black and cold; but when we ran out upon it we found it hot yet, to the feet, and it was likewise riven with crevices which revealed the underlying fires gleaming vindictively. A neighboring cauldron was threatening to overflow, and this added to the dubiousness of the situation. So the native guides refused to continue the venture, and then every body deserted except a stranger named Marlette. He said he had been in the crater a dozen times in daylight and believed he could find his way through it at night. He thought that a run of three hundred yards would carry us over the hottest part of the floor and leave us our shoe-soles. His pluck gave me back-bone. We took one lantern and instructed the guides to hang the other to the roof of the look-out house to serve as a beacon for us in case we got lost, and then the party started back up the precipice and Marlette and I made our run. We skipped over the hot floor and over the red crevices with brisk dispatch and reached the cold lava safe but with pretty warm feet. Then we took things leisurely and comfortably, jumping tolerably wide and probably bottomless chasms, and threading our way through picturesque lava upheavals with considerable confidence. When we got fairly away from the cauldrons of boiling fire, we seemed to be in a gloomy desert, and a suffocatingly dark one, surrounded by dim walls that seemed to tower to the sky. The only cheerful objects were the glinting stars high overhead.

By and by Marlette shouted "Stop!" I never stopped quicker in my life. I asked what the matter was. He said we were out of the path. He said we must not try to go on till we found it again, for we were surrounded with beds of rotten lava through which we could easily break and plunge down a thousand feet. I thought eight hundred would answer for me, and was about to say so when Marlette partly proved his statement by accidentally crushing through and disappearing to his arm-pits. He got out and we hunted for the path with the lantern. He said there was only one path and that it was but vaguely defined. We could not find it. The lava surface was all alike in the lantern light. But he was an ingenious man. He said it was not the lantern that had informed him that we were out of the path, but his *feet*. He had noticed a crisp grinding of fine lava-needles under his feet, and some instinct reminded him that in the path these were all worn away. So he put the lantern behind him, and began to search with his boots instead of his eyes. It was good sagacity. The first time his foot touched a surface that did not grind under it he announced that the trail was found again; and after that we kept up a sharp listening for the rasping sound and it always warned us in time.

It was a long tramp, but an exciting one. We reached the North Lake between ten and eleven o'clock, and sat down on a huge overhanging lava-shelf, tired but satisfied. The spectacle presented was worth coming double the distance to see. Under us, and stretching away before us, was a heaving sea of molten fire of seemingly limitless extent. The glare from it was so blinding that it was some time before we could bear to look upon it steadily. It was like gazing at the sun at noon-day, except that the glare was not quite so white. At unequal distances all around the shores of the lake were nearly white-hot chimneys or hollow drums of lava, four or five feet high, and up through them were bursting gorgeous sprays of lava-gouts and gem spangles, some white, some red and some golden—a ceaseless bombardment, and one that fascinated the eye with its unapproachable splendor. The more distant jets, sparkling up through an intervening gossamer veil of vapor, seemed miles away; and the further the curving ranks of fiery fountains receded, the more fairy-like and beautiful they appeared.

Now and then the surging bosom of the lake under our noses would calm down ominously and seem to be gathering strength for an enterprise; and then all of a sudden a red dome of lava of the bulk of an ordinary dwelling would heave itself aloft like an escaping balloon, then burst asunder, and out of its heart would flit a pale-green film of vapor, and float upward and vanish in the darkness—a released soul soaring homeward from captivity with the damned, no doubt. The crashing plunge of the ruined dome into the lake again would send a world of seething billows lashing against the shores and shaking the foundations of our perch. By and by, a loosened mass of the hanging shelf we sat on tumbled into the lake, jarring the surroundings like an earthquake and delivering a suggestion that may have been intended for a hint, and may not. We did not wait to see.

We got lost again on our way back, and were more than an hour hunting for the path. We were where we could see the beacon lantern at the look-out house at the time, but thought it was a star and paid no attention to it. We reached the hotel at two o'clock in the morning pretty well fagged out.

Kilauea never overflows its vast crater, but bursts a passage for its lava through the mountain side when relief is necessary, and then the destruction is fearful. About 1840 it rent its overburdened stomach and sent a broad river of fire careening down to the sea, which swept away forests, huts, plantations and every thing else that lay in its path. The stream was *five miles broad*, in places, and *two hundred feet deep*, and the distance it traveled was forty miles. It tore up and bore away acre-patches of land on its bosom like rafts—rocks, trees and all intact. At night the red glare was visible a hundred miles at sea; and at a distance of forty miles fine print could be read at midnight. The atmosphere was poisoned with sulphurous vapors and choked with falling ashes, pumice stones and cinders; countless columns of smoke rose up and blended together in a tumbled canopy that hid the heavens and glowed with a ruddy flush reflected from the fires below; here and there jets of lava sprang hundreds of feet into the air and burst into rocket-sprays that returned to earth in a crimson rain; and all the while the laboring mountain shook with Nature's great palsy, and voiced its distress in moanings and the muffled booming of subterranean thunders.

Fishes were killed for twenty miles along the shore, where the lava entered the sea. The earthquakes caused some loss of human life, and a prodigious tidal wave swept inland, carrying every thing before it and drowning a number of natives. The devastation consummated along the route traversed by the river of lava was complete and incalculable.

Only a Pompeii and a Herculaneum were needed at the foot of Kilauea to make the story of the irruption immortal.

Chapter XIII

We rode horseback all around the island of Hawaii (the crooked road making the distance two hundred miles), and enjoyed the journey very much. We were more than a week making the trip, because our Kanaka horses would not go by a house or a hut without stopping—whip and spur could not alter their minds about it, and so we finally found that it economized time to let them have their way. Upon inquiry the mystery was explained: the natives are such thorough-going gossips that they never pass a house without stopping to swap news, and consequently their horses learn to regard that sort of thing as an essential part of the whole duty of man, and his salvation not to be compassed without it. However, at a former crisis of my life I had once taken an aristocratic young lady out driving, behind a horse that had just retired from a long and honorable career as the moving impulse of a milk wagon, and so this present experience awoke a reminiscent sadness in me in place of the exasperation more natural to the occasion. I remembered how helpless I was that day, and how humiliated; how ashamed I was of having intimated to the girl that I had always owned the horse and was accustomed to grandeur;

how hard I tried to appear easy, and even vivacious, under suffering that was consuming my vitals; how placidly and maliciously the girl smiled, and kept on smiling, while my hot blushes baked themselves into a permanent blood-pudding in my face; how the horse ambled from one side of the street to the other and waited complacently before every third house two minutes and a quarter while I belabored his back and reviled him in my heart; how I tried to keep him from turning corners, and failed; how I moved heaven and earth to get him out of town, and did not succeed; how he traversed the entire settlement and delivered imaginary milk at a hundred and sixty-two different domiciles, and how he finally brought up at a dairy depot and refused to budge further, thus rounding and completing the revealment of what the plebeian service of his life had been; how, in eloquent silence, I walked the girl home, and how, when I took leave of her, her parting remark scorched my soul and appeared to blister me all over: she said that my horse was a fine, capable animal, and I must have taken great comfort in him in my time—but that if I would take along some milk-tickets next time, and appear to deliver them at the various halting places, it might expedite his movements a little. There was a coolness between us after that.

In one place in the island of Hawaii, we saw a laced and ruffled cataract of limpid water leaping from a sheer precipice fifteen hundred feet high; but that sort of scenery finds its stanchest ally in the arithmetic rather than in spectacular effect. If one desires to be so stirred by a poem of Nature wrought in the happily commingled graces of picturesque rocks, glimpsed distances, foliage, color, shifting lights and shadows, and falling water, that the tears almost come into his eyes so potent is the charm exerted, he need not go away from America to enjoy such an experience. The Rainbow Fall, in Watkins Glen (N. Y.), on the Erie railway, is an example. It would recede into pitiable insignificance if the callous tourist drew an arithmetic on it; but left to compete for the horrors simply on scenic grace and beauty—the grand, the august and the sublime being barred the contest—it could challenge the old world and the new to produce its peer.

In one locality, on our journey, we saw some horses that had been born and reared on top of the mountains, above the range of running water, and consequently they had never drank that fluid in their lives, but had been always accustomed to quenching their thirst by eating dew-laden or shower-wetted leaves. And now it was destructively funny to see them sniff suspiciously at a pail of water, and then put in their noses and try to take a *bite* out of the fluid, as if it were a solid. Finding it liquid, they would snatch away their heads and fall to trembling, snorting and showing other evidences of fright. When they became convinced at last that the water was friendly and harmless, they thrust in their noses up to their eyes, brought out a mouthful of the water, and proceeded to *chew* it complacently. We saw a man coax, kick and spur one of them five or ten minutes before he could make it cross a running stream. It spread its nostrils, distended its eyes and trembled all over, just as horses customarily do in the presence of a serpent—and for aught I know it thought the crawling stream *was* a serpent.

In due course of time our journey came to an end at Kawaehae (usually pronounced To-a-*hi*—and before we find fault with this elaborate orthographical method of arriving at such an unostentatious result, let us lop off the *ugh* from our word "though"). I made this horseback trip on a mule. I paid ten dollars for him at Kau (Kah-oo), added four to get him shod, rode him two hundred miles, and then sold him for fifteen dollars. I mark the circumstance with a white stone (in the absence of chalk—for I never saw a white stone that a body could mark anything with, though out of respect for the ancients I have tried it often enough); for up to that day and date it was the first strictly commercial transaction I had ever entered into, and come out winner. We returned to Honolulu, and from thence sailed to the island of Maui, and spent several weeks there very pleasantly. I still remember, with a sense of indolent luxury, a picnicking excursion up a romantic gorge there, called the Iao Valley. The trail lay along the edge of a brawling stream in the bottom of the gorge—a shady route, for it was well roofed with the verdant domes of forest trees. Through openings in the foliage we glimpsed picturesque scenery that revealed ceaseless changes and new charms with every step of our progress. Perpendicular walls from one to three thousand feet high guarded the way, and were sumptuously plumed with varied foliage, in places, and in places swathed in waving ferns. Passing shreds of cloud trailed their shadows across these shining fronts, mottling them with blots; billowy masses of white vapor hid the turreted summits, and far above the vapor swelled a background of gleaming green crags and cones that came and went, through the veiling mists, like islands drifting in a fog; sometimes the cloudy curtain descended till half the canyon wall was hidden, then shredded gradually away till only airy glimpses of the ferny front appeared through it— then swept aloft and left it glorified in the sun again. Now and then, as our position changed, rocky bastions swung out from the wall, a mimic ruin of castellated ramparts and crumbling towers clothed with mosses and hung with garlands of swaying vines, and as we moved on they swung back again and hid themselves once more in the foliage. Presently a verdure-clad needle of stone, a thousand feet high, stepped out from behind a corner, and mounted guard over the mysteries of the valley. It seemed to me that if Captain Cook needed a monument, here was one ready made—therefore, why not put up his sign here, and sell out the venerable cocoanut stump?

But the chief pride of Maui is her dead volcano of Halea-kala—which means, translated, "the house of the sun." We climbed a thousand feet up the side of this isolated colossus one afternoon; then camped, and next day climbed the remaining nine thousand feet, and anchored on the summit, where we built a fire and froze and roasted by turns, all night. With the first pallor of dawn we got up and saw things that were new to us. Mounted on a commanding pinnacle, we watched Nature work her silent wonders. The sea was spread abroad on every hand, its tumbled surface seeming only wrinkled and dimpled in the distance. A broad valley below appeared like an ample checker-board, its velvety green sugar plantations alternating with dun squares of barrenness and groves of trees diminished to mossy tufts. Beyond the valley were mountains picturesquely grouped together; but bear in mind, we fancied that we were looking *up* at these things—not down. We seemed to sit in the bottom of a symmetrical bowl ten thousand feet deep, with the valley and the skirting sea lifted away into the sky above us! It was curious; and not only curious, but aggravating; for it was having our trouble all for nothing, to climb ten thousand feet toward heaven and then have to look *up* at our scenery. However, we had to be content with it and make the best of it; for, all we could do we could not coax our landscape down out of the clouds. Formerly, when I had read an article in which Poe treated of this singular fraud perpetrated upon the eye by isolated great altitudes, I had looked upon the matter as an invention of his own fancy.

I have spoken of the outside view—but we had an inside view, too. That was the yawning dead crater, into which we now and then tumbled rocks, half as large as a barrel, from our perch, and saw them go careering down the almost perpendicular sides, bounding three hundred feet at a jump; kicking up dust-clouds wherever they struck; diminishing to our view as they sped farther into distance; growing invisible, finally, and only betraying their course by faint little puffs of dust; and coming to a halt at last in the bottom of the abyss, two thousand five hundred feet down from where they started! It was magnificent sport. We wore ourselves out at it.

The crater of Vesuvius, as I have before remarked, is a modest pit about a thousand feet deep and three thousand in circumference; that of Kilauea is somewhat deeper, and *ten miles* in circumference. But what are either of them compared to the vacant stomach of Haleakala! I will not offer any figures of my own, but give official ones—those of Commander Wilkes, U. S. N., who surveyed it and testifies that it is *twenty-seven miles in circumference!* If it had a level bottom it would make a fine site for a city like London. It must have afforded a spectacle worth contemplating in the old days when its furnace gave full rein to their anger.

Presently vagrant white clouds came drifting along, high over the sea and the valley; then they came in couples and groups; then in imposing squadrons; gradually joining their forces they banked themselves solidly together, a thousand feet under us, and *totally shut out land and ocean*—not a vestige of *anything* was left in view but just a little of the rim of the crater, circling away from the pinnacle whereon we sat (for a ghostly procession of wanderers from the filmy hosts without had drifted through a chasm in the crater wall and filed round and round, and gathered and sunk and blended together till the abyss was stored to the brim with a fleecy fog). Thus banked, motion ceased, and silence reigned. Clear to the horizon, league on league, the snowy floor stretched without a break—not level, but in rounded folds, with shallow creases between, and with here and there stately piles of vapory architecture lifting themselves aloft out of the common plain—some near at hand, some in the middle distances, and others relieving the monotony of the remote solitudes. There was little conversation, for the impressive scene overawed speech. I felt like the Last Man, neglected of the judgment, and left pinnacled in mid-heaven, a forgotten relic of a vanished world.

While the hush yet brooded, the messengers of the coming resurrection appeared in the East. A growing warmth suffused the horizon, and soon the sun emerged and looked out over the cloud-waste, flinging bars of ruddy light across it; staining it's folds and billow-caps with blushes, purpling the shaded troughs between, and glorifying the massy vapor-palaces and cathedrals with a wasteful splendor of all blendings and combinations of rich coloring.

It was the sublimest spectacle I ever witnessed, and I think the memory of it will remain with me always.

Illustrations

The Hawaii that Mark Twain visited.

Note: While some of the photos and illustrations are dated before or after Twain's 1866 visit, the sights had changed slightly, if at all.

Pa'u riders, a common sight in 1860's Honolulu. Lithograph by C. Thornam, Baker-Van Dyke Collection.

Honolulu, capital of the Sandwich Islands. Engraving by Charles De Varigny, Baker-Van Dyke Collection.

The view towards Diamond Head from downtown Honolulu. Baker-Van Dyke Collection.

Diamond Head and eastern Honolulu from the tower of the Catholic church on Fort Street. The building in front of Kawaiahao Church is Iolani Palace. From a lithograph by Paul Emment, Baker-Van Dyke Collection.

The Court House, home of the legislature and gala events. By Chase, Baker-Van Dyke Collection.

Kawaiahao Church. By Chase, Baker-Van Dyke Collection.

The business center of downtown Honolulu. Baker-Van Dyke Collection.

Residence of Princess Victoria Kamamalu, later the Royal Palace to be replaced by Iolani Palace. Stangenwald, Baker-Van Dyke Collection.

The Village of Waikiki. Engraving by Charles De Varigny. Baker-Van Dyke Collection.

The King's House in the village of Waikiki, the residence of Kamehameha V, later the site of the Royal Hawaiian Hotel. Engraving by Charles De Varigny, Baker-Van Dyke Collection.

Surfing in Hawaii. Engraving by Charles De Varigny, Baker-Van Dyke Collection.

Hula Dancers. Baker-Van Dyke Collection.

Men in canoes. Bishop Museum.

Pounding poi. Baker-Van Dyke Collection.

Selling taro. Baker-Van Dyke Collection.

The south Kona landing. By Gonsalves, Baker-Van Dyke Collection.

Hale o Keawe, the City of Refuge. Baker-Van Dyke Collection.

Large grass house in Honolulu. Engraving by C. Skogman, Baker-Van Dyke Collection.

Kealakekua Bay. Baker-Van Dyke Collection.

Captain Cook. Baker-Van Dyke Collection.

The death of Captain Cook. Hawaii State Archives.

Copper plate at Cook's monument.
Bishop Museum.

Captain Cook monument. By Chase, Baker-Van Dyke Collection.

Kamehameha I. By Choris, Baker-Van Dyke Collection.

Kaahumanu. Baker-Van Dyke Collection.

Prominent Hawaiian aliʻi: **Top of stairs**—*William Pitt Kinau, Bernice Pauahi Bishop.* **At balcony**—*Lydia K. Dominis, Kamehameha V.* **Stairs**—*Kalama, widow of Kamehamea III, Honorable David Kalakaua, Matais Kekuanaoa.* **Bottom, left to right**—*Mrs. Kapiolani, wife of David Kalakaua, nurse to the young Prince of Hawaii, Queen Emma, Kamehameha IV, P. Nahaolelua, Victoria Kamamalu. Engraving by Charles De Varigny, Baker-Van Dyke Collection.*

TALES OF THE PACIFIC

JACK LONDON
Stories of Hawaii $4.95
South Sea Tales $4.95
Captain David Grief (originally A Son of the Sun) $4.95
The Mutiny of the "Elsinore" $4.95

HAWAII
Remember Pearl Harbor by Blake Clark $3.95
Kona by Marjorie Sinclair $3.95
The Spell of Hawaii $4.95
A Hawaiian Reader $4.95
The Golden Cloak by Antoinette Withington $3.95
Russian Flag Over Hawaii by Darwin Teilhet 3.95
Teller of Tales by Eric Knudsen $4.95
Myths and Legends of Hawaii by W.D. Westervelt $3.95
Mark Twain in Hawaii $4.95
The Legends and Myths of Hawaii by Kalakaua $6.95
Hawaii's Story by Hawaii's Queen $6.95
Rape in Paradise by Theon Wright $4.95
The Betrayal of Liliuokalani $6.95
The Wild Wind by Marjorie Sinclair $4.95

SOUTH SEAS LITERATURE
The Trembling of a Leaf by W. Somerset Maugham $3.95
Rogues of the South Seas by A. Grove Day $3.95
The Book of Puka-Puka by Robert Dean Frisbie $3.95
The Lure of Tahiti, ed. by A. Grove Day $3.95
The Blue of Capricorn by Eugene Burdick $3.95
Horror in Paradise, ed. by A. Grove Day and Bacil F. Kirtley $4.95
Best South Sea Stories, ed. by A. Grove Day $4.95
The Forgotten One by James Norman Hall $3.95

TRAVEL, BIOGRAPHY, ANTHROPOLOGY
Manga Reva by Robert Lee Eskridge $3.95
Coronado's Quest by A. Grove Day $3.95
Love in the South Seas by Bengt Danielsson $3.95
Home from the Sea: Robert Louis Stevenson in Samoa by Richard A.
   Bermann $3.95
The Norhoff-Hall Story: In Search of Paradise by Paul L. Briand, $4.95
The Fatal Impact by Alan Moorehead $3.95
Claus Spreckels: The Sugar King in Hawaii by Jacob Adler $3.95
A Dream of Islands by Gavan Daws $4.95

———————

Orders should be sent to Mutual Publishing Co.
2055 N. King St., Honolulu, HI 96819. Add $2.00 handling for the first
book and $1.00 for each book thereafter. For airmail add $2.00 per book.